MW00954936

Greed to Grace: The Golden Handcuffs

By
Daniel D. Grauer

Dedication

This book is dedicated to those I hurt the most through my inexcusable decision-making, ignoring God's presence in my life, and selfishness, pride, and sheer stupidity. It is dedicated to those that were most loyal during this entire ordeal: my wife, best friend, and guardian angel, Joyce, and the most faithful of companions, my black lab, K.C. (October 1994 – August 2008).

Introduction

It's been fourteen years, but not a day goes by that I don't feel the guilt, the anguish, and the embarrassment of my past. I continually look over my shoulder to see if my past has left me --- but it hasn't, nor will it, ever! God can forgive, but society does not; as a result, I cannot forgive myself because I am not allowed to forget.

As you read this book, please, take note of the temptations, the sins, and the human weaknesses. Many of us have succumbed to similar moral misjudgments and disregard for values, but then again, maybe not to the extent which I crossed the line.

The two most vivid and effective analogies I can use to describe this period of my life are: close your eyes and imagine a snowball, tightly packed, cold, wet and heavy, rolling downward from high a top the tallest mountain. Slowly at first, but with one nudge after another, the snowball gets a little bigger and rolls a little farther. Soon, the snowball is rolling on its own, gathering speed as it proceeds down the mountainside, all the time getting bigger and bigger and bigger and moving faster and faster. As the snowball increases in size and speed, it dislodges more snowpack from the mountainside and is now three times its original size. Less than one-quarter way down the side of the mountain, a small, harmless snowball has turned into an uncontrollable avalanche, destroying everything in its path without regard to those affected by the destruction.

Now, close your eyes and imagine a totally blue sky, not a cloud can be detected for miles. A seemingly endless valley of rolling hills covered with lush green grass, wild flowers of every kind, and trees with too many shades of green to count. In the center of the valley is a lake. The lake is clear and shimmers in sunlight, so bright you have to shield your eyes to see the deep, dark blue color of the water. This gift was created by the hand of God. Only He could be so detailed, ornate, and complex, yet so loving and caring. God's peace, calmness, and serenity surround the lake.

Are you there in your mind yet? Bend over and pick up a round stone, about the size of a baseball. Throw the stone high into the air, out over the water. Watch closely as it descends and splashes into the water. See the ripple? See the waves that permeate from the center of the splash in all directions? Watch, as the resulting waves seem to keep going and going until finally the waves, once again, smooth out as they approach the shoreline.

Etch these analogies into your mind as you read this book. I assure you, all will become clear. These analogies can apply to much of our lives, including the many complications, trials, and tribulations we experience. I truly hope and pray that you learn from my mistakes.

This book is based on a real-life event. The conversations, meeting dates, and specifics are only memories and are not literal in every context.

The following pages are my perceptions, thoughts, and memories only, however flawed they may be. I have changed the names of those persons who were a part of my life during this snapshot in my life, except for immediate family members. I want to protect them from any further embarrassment and humiliation.

To those I disappointed, embarrassed, humiliated, angered, and hurt, I truly apologize. I can only ask your forgiveness!

Chapter 1

The sudden blaring of the alarm clock startled me. The sun was just beginning to peek through the window; bright rays of sunshine created shadows on the wall that sent a shiver down my spine. I could hear the wind whistling through the trees as if singing a warning of what was to come.

Sleep had not come easily for quite some time. Nightmares of misrepresentations, claims fraud, and mail fraud haunted my mind each time my eyes closed. Four hours of sleep at night had become the norm instead of the exception.

I knew this was going to be the day, the day I had dreaded for a very long time. My stomach hurt as though someone had taken a glowing, red-hot fireplace poker and rammed it through, searing the flesh, trying to reach my spine. I felt sick to my stomach, trying not to vomit with each breath of the morning. My head felt like a basketball that had spent years being dribbled up and down the court, only to end up lopsided, deflated, and worn out.

I got dressed in the usual business casual requirement. I slipped into a pair of black wrinkle-free Dockers, a silver and white striped dress shirt, black socks, and black slip-on shoes. I stared at my railroad identification badge, knowing I would not clip it to my belt ever again, and still, even at this moment, I dared to tell no one . . .

My wife and kids were just beginning to get up and around. The usual hustle and bustle of a working family was taking hold. Listening would bring the sounds of arguments surrounding what was acceptable and what was not to be worn to school---was too much belly showing---or the frustrations of a bad hair day. The kids never seemed to find whatever it was they were looking for. Either they hadn't seen it, or when they did, someone else had taken it. Getting the beds made and teeth brushed was always a daily struggle, with today being no exception. How unimportant that all seemed.

I grabbed a mug from the cupboard and poured the coffee too quickly, spilling more than went into the cup. This day was not going to be good. Walking to the front door to retrieve the newspaper prompted Smokey, our cat, to entwine himself into my legs with each step. His constant "meowing and whining," reinforced his attempted communication of hunger. He considered himself as important as any other member of the family. Looking down, I saw cat hair up and down my pants legs; today it made me smile.

Reaching for the front door, I gave Smokey a friendly boot in the rear so he wouldn't get out as I grabbed for the newspaper lying on the front porch. Closing the front door, I slipped the rubber band off the rolled-up paper and half-heartedly shot it at him. I obviously insulted him, as he raced toward the basement.

Tossing the newspaper on the dining room table, I decided to check my e-mail. Attempting to log into the railroad network confirmed my fears: "Access Denied." My anxiety level jumped a couple of notches as my heart rate drastically increased. I reasoned that maybe it was merely a technical or network problem, but in my heart, I knew the truth.

I logged onto AOL and saw the never-ending "Spam" e-mails I received daily. I looked at several of them, not really reading or comprehending, deleting them almost as quickly as they were opened. An e-mail from my brother caught my attention, so I opened it.

Dan –
I hadn't talked with you since Christmas. It was good to see you and the family. I am going to be in Council Bluffs, working at some point over the next few weeks, and I thought I would take you and the family out to dinner. Let me know . . . Love –

"Love!" Tears began to well up; how could I tell them? If he only knew, he might change his mind. The tears ran down my cheeks. I shut down the computer and moved to the dining room table in an effort to slow down my emotional roller coaster.

I casually glanced through the newspaper, not really reading or concentrating on any one article. I looked up and right into the hazel eyes of my wife. I immediately glanced away for fear of breaking down. I just knew she could read my mind. She knew me better than I knew myself, and had asked numerous times over the past weeks, "What's wrong?" Fear boiled in the pit of my stomach. Did she know? Had she suspected all along? What will I say? What will I tell my kids, my parents, and my family? Numerous times over the past weeks, the easy way out of this atrocity---ending my life---had crossed my mind.

Grabbing my coffee, I walked toward the patio door. The coffee burned my lips as I stared out the back sliding door window at the most loyal of family members, our dog. K.C., named after the Kansas City Chiefs by my son, was a young black lab, always in the mood to play, to run, and to chase the ever-elusive squirrel or rabbit. The squirrels frustrated and teased him. They would come within a very short distance of his pen, stand up on their back legs, and chatter as if to say, "I know you can't get out of that pen and I am going to sit here just to drive you crazy." A sudden shiver down my spine forced me back to reality; I wondered if dogs ever had bad days. Today I would have given anything to change places with him.

It was January 15, 2001; the sun was shining bright and it was unseasonably warm in Omaha, Nebraska. A cool wind signaled that winter was not yet over. A light dusting of snow had covered the ground, but small clumps of grass could be seen stretching for the warmth of the sun. Most of the leaves on the trees had long since fallen to the ground, but many were still clinging on, fighting not to let go. I looked at my wristwatch: 7:15 a.m., time to head toward work. My stomach wrenched again with pain. My heart and my head knew this would be the longest day of my life and the last of a long career.

Chapter 2

Traffic wasn't bad on this Monday morning. My mind was everywhere, except on driving. A myriad of thoughts raced through my mind. Omaha was a wonderful place to live, and a person could be anywhere in the city or surrounding areas in twenty – thirty minutes. The people here actually smile, wave, and extend a hearty, "good morning." Entertainment was bountiful and easy to find. Located along the Missouri River allowed Omaha a variety of seasons and weather conditions. One old adage always seemed to hold true: "If you didn't like the weather in Nebraska, just wait a few hours, it will change." I loved Omaha, but could Omaha ever again love me?

I thought about my father's forty-four-year career with the railroad: only one sick day, with the exception of a severe on-duty personal injury that took him from work for almost two years. Norman, or Bubba among co-workers, was without a doubt, one of the most dedicated, respected, and loyal employees the railroad had ever hired. Dad's work ethic and morals were beyond reproach. Growing up, I recall dad getting called to work at all hours of the night due to train derailments; not once did he shirk his duties or show any animosity toward his employer.

When I started my railroad career in 1979, I was working side by side with my dad. I don't think I ever told him at the time, but that was one of the true highlights of my life. He knew more about the inner workings of mechanical freight cars than any manual I had been given. Dad was certified by the American Association of Railroads as a freight car inspector. This was no easy task. His very detailed and thorough mechanical inspections often times revealed defects overlooked by others. I learned a great deal from dad. I was extremely proud of him and the example he had set. I was a third-generation railroader . . . but not for long. Where had I made a wrong turn? What precipitated the mess that was about to unfold? What was I thinking? How could I tell him the truth?

A car horn blasted me back to reality. I looked in the rear-view mirror to see my secretary's great, big, "I gotcha," smile. She was a very special lady, contracted with the railroad through one of the many "temp" agencies used to cut cost. Vickie had fought and won the battle with cancer at a very young age. Her attitude toward life was always so bright, positive, and upbeat. Vickie was not a small or petite lady, nor would she ever be on the cover of a Glamour magazine; yet she was one of the most beautiful people I ever had the opportunity to interact with; her beauty truly came from within.

I thought about how lucky I had been to have Vickie as a secretary. She was beyond efficient; her organizational, business management, and communication skills were extremely high. I know that a majority of my own successes would not have come about had it not been for her expertise. She was always telling me about her kids, her church, and her music.

As I continued in my little dream world, it dawned on me how much unconditional love and trust Vickie had in God. I made a mental note of that.

Bang! Bang! Bang!

I looked in the driver's side mirror of my truck once again to see, who else but Vickie, pounding on the side of my truck and yelling, "Hey, Lieutenant Dan, Lieutenant Dan, WAKE UP!" I smiled; Vickie had started calling me Lieutenant Dan shortly after seeing the movie *Forrest Gump*, and the nickname caught on amongst those who worked for me.

I opened the door of my truck to step our and began to turn when once again I heard, "Hey, Lieutenant Dan, what's the matter? Are you all right? Not sick are you?"

Maybe I should just call in sick and go home. I wasn't ready for today. Was this the right decision? Could I actually go through with this? Looking into the always smiling eyes of Miss Vickie, I thought, *how on earth could I face and accept the consequences of my actions?*

"Hey, Vick, why are you always so chipper and happy? I really hate people like you."

"Lots to be thankful for," came the immediate response. "Wanna hear about it?"

"No. Vick don't start on me today, PLEASE!"

The walk to the entrance was less than twenty yards away and yet it seemed like miles. I punched in the security code and held the door open for Vickie. I quickly stepped inside the door and stopped.

I really could go back home. I wouldn't have to do this today. No, today is the day and the time is now. I began to move down the hallway. I looked down at my shoes, as my feet seemed as heavy as concrete blocks.

"Hey, I know you're older'n dirt Lieutenant Dan, but I got work to do. Can ya'll walk any faster?" Vickie took off down the hallway, like a rabbit singing to herself the whole way.

I took one more step and tears began to stream down my face again. I walked very slowly, inching my way down the hallway noticing, for what seemed like the very first time, the many things I had never taken the time to see in a pathway that I had walked literally thousands of times.

A picture about twenty feet down the hallway caught my eye. I never saw that wall hanging before. The rainbow in the painting poked through the silver and black storm clouds and stretched in an almost perfect arc, like a piece of brightly colored ribbon streaming to the ground. On the ground an endless blanket of flowers enclosed the rainbow as it faded into nothingness.

Today was going to be anything but typical. I seemed more aware of my surroundings and the detail that encompassed all of my senses. As I moved down the hallway a sudden surge of nausea overcame me. I sprinted into the first stall of the men's bathroom, just in time for retching, pain, and endless shaking to begin. Getting sick had almost become routine. After a few minutes, I stood in front of the mirror and splashed cold water on my face, looking for any little bit of relief for what was to come. A glance in the mirror revealed a face I didn't know. I was sweating profusely and, at this moment in time, very glad no one else was in the restroom.

As I approached my office door, I saw my boss sitting in a chair just outside, staring at the floor as if he were trying to find something in the carpet at his feet. Ron was dedicated to all aspects of his life, approximately 5' 9" tall and tremendously athletic. I had never met someone so dedicated to total physical fitness: running, weight lifting, kickboxing, baseball, and an almost professional ability toward golf. As I stopped and looked at his face, I could see only anguish and disappointment. Bent at the waist, his elbows rested on his thighs, and his hands were folded together as if he were praying; maybe he was.

This confirmed what was to come, and most certainly explained not being able to log into the computer system; I was about to be terminated.

Chapter 3

Another step and Ron looked up at me. His eyes were red; had he been crying? I did my best to give a jolly, "Hello," but what came out of my mouth was barely audible and I was certainly anything but jolly. Our eyes met only briefly; for the first time in my career, I felt the deep disappointment and sadness I had created.

Ron finally spoke. "Dan, we need to meet with the corporate auditors first thing this morning, before you even get settled in." I glanced at the door and wondered if my access badge had been deactivated and if the personal items in my office had already been put in boxes.

Ron looked away and started toward the elevator. He stopped and stared straight ahead at the elevator buttons, not saying another word nor finding any reason to turn around. I followed, purposely staying behind to avoid looking any further into his eyes.

"Where are we meeting?"

"In their office," came his short, military type of reply.

I must have given the deer in the headlights look to Ron. After what seemed like a very long time, he stepped in front of me.

"You . . . O.K.?" he whispered.

"This is the end, isn't it?" I asked.

He turned on his heels and walked away.

"God, when we decided to do this, you told me you'd be there by my side. I need you now."

Once again, I followed Ron down the hallway toward the elevators. I put my coat back on and zipped it up, despite the fact I was sweating profusely. The "ding" of the elevator arriving on the floor sounded as I picked up the briefcase I had left on the chair by my office door, and moved inside the waiting elevator car.

The auditors' office was in a building, a little over a block down the street. I tried to stay one step behind and to the left of Ron, avoiding any uncomfortable glance or conversation. I only needed a short glance to know that Ron had lost all respect for me as an employee and as a friend, and rightfully so.

The walk should have taken only minutes but, like everything happening today, it seemed an eternity.

"Almighty God, during the past months I have had many ups and downs; I have told countless lies and committed many, many sins. I have not been, in any way, the person you created me to be. Please, forgive me! Please, give me the courage and strength to make it through today. God, I am out of options here. HELP ME!" I begged as walk continued.

I don't know if it was the nervousness or just being so scared, but I must have been praying aloud, or at least loud enough for Ron to hear me. He stopped, put his hand on my shoulder with a firm grip, looked me in the eyes, and said, "I'm sorry." I had no clue to what he was referring; I was the one that should be apologizing.

The elevator reached the fourth floor. I stepped out behind Ron and turned to the right, looking down the infamous corridor of corporate auditors, that part of the company everyone loved to hate. Sitting on a chair just outside the conference room was another familiar face. I had worked with the railroad's special agent office on numerous occasions in the past. They were a highly trained and efficient corporate police force, utilized in all aspects of internal law enforcement. On this occasion, Larry was here because of me, not to assist me.

Larry and I had worked together on multiple personal injury cases, crossing accident investigations, and train derailments. Our work often resulted in the development, presentation, and implementation of safety programs that positively impacted the work environment at the railroad. I recalled Larry sharing stories of his past wherein he investigated and assisted in the prosecution of employees caught in fraudulent behaviors or other criminal situations. He would always tell me how sad it made him to do so, but Larry was dedicated, loyal, and truly liked his job

"Hey, Larry," I barely whispered.

A nod of the head and a very sullen, "Dan," was his only response.

Like Ron, I could see and sense the disappointment, the sadness, and the disbelief that simply could not be hidden. I swallowed hard and kept right on walking as my emotional roller coaster hit another wave. I was certain that Larry had utilized all his skills and talents in working on my investigation. He was good. I was also equally certain he didn't like the results he obtained this time. I had been with the railroad long enough to know that Larry would escort me off railroad property at the conclusion of my meeting. What would I say? Could I face him? What plausible explanation could there be? What was to explain? I had lost another coworker and friend.

I must have stopped walking, because when I looked up, Ron was holding open the door of the conference room. As I entered the room, I looked at the plush furnishings. A dark mahogany conference table occupied a majority of the oval-shaped room; it was big enough for twelve overstuffed chairs on rollers to be neatly arranged around its edge. A six-drawer, lateral credenza that perfectly matched the table sat under the window on the far wall. At the far end of the room, mounted on the wall, was a multipurpose training aid that contained a dry erase board that doubled as a video screen when needed. Every electronic device needed for any type of video, audio, or visual presentation was there. Hanging on the walls were various framed photographs depicting the history of the railroad.

From the other side of the room, an unfamiliar voice said, "Have a seat, Mr. Grauer." I turned and looked into the strictly business-like eyes of the railroad's chief auditor. Victor had a reputation that paralleled no other financial manager. He was thorough, detailed, and painstakingly organized. Victor was simply regarded as "the best" when it came to tracking and following the money trail.

"Shall we begin?" he asked in a voice that almost seemed pleased.

"God, help me and forgive me," I prayed.

"What?" he asked. "Yes, well, let's get this over with. Mr. Grauer, do you know why you are here?"

"Well, I assume you have completed the corporate audit of my files. I also assume that you located the separate file and all the documents associated with that file underneath my desk in the black attaché that is now sitting in front of you. Finally, I will assume that you have numerous questions to ask regarding that particular file."

"Yes, Mr. Grauer, I do indeed! However, before we go too far, I would like your permission to tape-record this meeting."

"Fine." The eerie quietness in the room as the tape recorder was turned on was almost too much to bear.

"Mr. Grauer, our team has completed an audit of the file in question. Was this particular claims file your responsibility and was it handled solely by you?"

"Yes, to both questions."

"Thank you. Our team has discovered numerous discrepancies that fall outside the claims-handling guidelines and financial guidelines established within railroad procedure. I have a listing of these discrepancies, and I would like to review them one item at a time for clarification."

"Okey-dokey!" I couldn't believe those words rolled out of my mouth, especially at a time like this. "Okey-dokey!" What was that? By the look in Victor's eyes, he saw no humor in my answer either.

"Item number one, Mr. Grauer. Please look at copies of the two receipts I am handing you. One is for a motel stay and the other for gas. They are dated months after the financial settlement of this personal injury claim. Why did you choose to reimburse them?"

"As I recall, the initial settlement covered lost wages in the past, pain and suffering, and future wage loss calculated to present value. Additionally, I chose to assist this claimant in relocation from Nebraska to Arkansas and agreed to cover all reasonable expenses related to this on-duty personal injury. The expense receipts you have handed me were for travel related to ongoing medical treatment for this injury." I thought I sounded very convincing and justified, but both my brain and heart knew that what I had said were lies.

"Fine, Mr. Grauer, let's move on. There appear to be numerous reimbursements, some of which I am sure you can explain and justify, but a golf cart?"

I was ready to spin yet another yarn about how, due to the injury and the resulting fourteen total surgeries to his elbows, hands, and shoulders, arthritis had spread throughout his lower extremities as well, making it impossible to walk long distances.

I opened my mouth to speak and what came out startled even me. I was overcome with a sensation that consumed me. An overwhelming contentment, peace, and calmness invaded my entire body. I closed my eyes momentarily and the image that formed in my mind was astounding. It was as if I was outside my own physical body, just watching to see what decision my mind would make. I was telling the Dan Grauer sitting at the conference table to listen to his heart, tell the truth, trust in the Lord as he had promised; it would be O.K.

"Yes, Mr. Grauer, we expect you to tell the truth."

I blinked and looked into the chief auditor's eyes, and wondered if he heard me talking to myself or whether I had truly spoken out loud to myself. My heart and soul had been telling me for a very long time, when I looked into a mirror, that it wasn't the Dan Grauer the Lord had created.

Inside the file carrier I had placed the entire paper trail of fraudulent activity: the claimant file itself, photocopies of all checks, or kickbacks, I had received over a two-year period, and all paperwork that I had changed, altered, photocopied, or used for justification of payments made to the claimant. I had placed statements in the attaché outlining the computer changes and cover-ups of all financial activity.

On two separate occasions, I had taken the file carrier out of the office to destroy the record trail and claimant file. In addition, on those two occasions, I could not follow through with the destruction, always bringing it back to my office and sitting it underneath my desk.

The nightmare was going to end now! It was time...

Chapter 4

I don't know where the courage and strength came from. I wasn't even listening to the words that came flowing from within me. I just sat back in the chair and began to speak, occasionally sobbing uncontrollably when referring to family and friends.

The tangled ball of string began to unravel and I was able to open the closed gates that had held so very many dark secrets. I released the build-up of lies, deceit, and fraud that had come to destroy the person, the father, the husband, and the employee.

I told of how the formation of the snowball began as a friendly gesture to reimburse expenses that were borderline in acceptability. I spoke about the claimant's expectations of money as the snowball rolled down the mountainside and gained momentum. I testified to having received "kickback" money from the claimant, including the emotional and psychological struggle in cashing the first check.

For a brief period, I had sat the snowball on the ground and just watched it. It didn't go away. I didn't move, but it didn't melt either. Another twinge of greed and I gave the snowball a nudge, then another and another. Months later, the snowball began rolling on its own, picking up speed, intensity, and size, and it continued down the mountainside. The love of money had me hooked. Satan reeled me in hook, line, and sinker. I testified to all the horrific and inexcusable decision-making with regard this particular claims file. I had chosen to accept money from a claimant; the more his expenses were reimbursed, the greater the amount of dollars that were "kicked back" in my direction. There was no verbal or written agreement; simply a bizarre type of non-questioning, yet, very illegal agreement.

When the claimant needed money, I would receive a stack of receipts in the mail, the receipts allegedly being related to ongoing medical treatment surrounding the personal injury claim. If I wanted money, I would send a check, insuring it was written for an amount small enough to avoid detection or arouse suspicion. When the claimant received a check written on a railroad bank draft, within two weeks I received money in the mail.

Three years later, what started as a friendly gesture to assist in additional medical expense reimbursement to a claimant and friend became a nightmare. In the snowball's journey down the mountainside, the intensity, power, and force had increased a hundredfold. The speed with which it moved accelerated in direct proportion to the descent. The volume of dislodged snowpack had become enormous; it had become an avalanche, destroying everything in its path, and it had not yet hit bottom.

For the first time in years, I was telling the truth regarding this claims file. The relief I felt was as if a load of bricks had lifted off my shoulders. I didn't realize at the time: God had just cut the weighted chain that was causing my descent into Satan's world.

Throughout my entire confession, I had been staring out the window. I blinked and looked around the room. With no exception, all those present were focused on looking down at the top of the conference table in front of them. I glanced toward Ron, my boss, and I thought for a second that I saw a lone tear trailing down his cheek.

"Anything else, Mr. Grauer?" asked a very quiet and significantly weakened chief auditor.

"Not that I can think of."

"One more question. How much total money did you receive from the claimant?"

"I truly have no idea, and at this point would not want to even guess."

"Mr. Grauer, I wish you knew how difficult this is for all of those people that have worked with you and come to respect your ability as a manager. You are being terminated as an employee. Please immediately surrender all corporate credit cards, identification, and any other railroad property in your possession. This information will be turned over to the U. S. Prosecutor for further handling. I would suggest you consult with an attorney. I would also ask that you sign two authorizations, one to release all of your banking and financial information and the other stating that the information you have provided us today was done without coercion and was purely voluntary on your part."

I felt extremely weak and nauseous. My arms felt like heavy weights. I began to read the authorizations and, once again, was overcome with a flood of tears. I picked up the pen to sign the authorizations and felt as though I were writing with a rock. I glanced down to see that the front of my shirt was damp and almost entirely covered in sweat and tears. A significant pile of Kleenex sat on the table in front of me.

This was it. I was a broken man; I would have welcomed the men in white jackets and a padded hospital room. My breathing was labored and heavy. I just wanted to rest, to sleep, just get some sleep. Never in a million years would I have dreamed the internal suffering, pain, and total disintegration something like this could cause.

Ron stood up and put his hand my shoulder. "Dan, I'm truly sorry. Take whatever time you need to compose yourself. If you need to call your wife or make any other phone calls, go ahead. There is a special agent outside the door to escort you off of railroad property when you are ready."

I don't know how long I sat with my face buried in my hands, weeping; time was of no consequence now. The entire gambit of emotions raced through my mind and body. One second I would be uncontrollably angry, and then scared, followed by thoughts of jumping through the window, and of total helplessness. I wanted to shake my fist and shout at God for allowing this to happen and, within the same few minutes, fall to my knees and beg for forgiveness, understanding, and compassion, but most of all peace.

I finally reached for the phone, picked up the receiver, and dialed my wife's work phone. "This is Sara. May I help you"?

Through all of the sniffles and tears I managed a barely audible, "Hey, honey."

I was greeted by silence. Anyone could have heard a pin drop. She knew. I didn't have to say a word.

"I've been fired, Sara. I told them everything. I had to. I couldn't do it anymore and look at myself in the mirror."

"What are we going to do?" came a soft, distant reply. I could tell that her mind had begun racing with what the future might hold.

"I don't know. We'll talk about it over the noon hour. I am going to call Tony, a very close friend in the railroad law department, and get a referral to a criminal attorney, and then I'll come home."

"O.K., I'll see you there," and she hung up the phone. Forever etched in my mind was the disappointment, the hurt, the fear, and the immediate barrier I heard in Sara's voice.

I briefly put the phone receiver down, picked it up again, and called Tony. "Tony, Dan Grauer, listen. If someone needed a really good criminal attorney in Omaha, who would you recommend?"

With only slight hesitation, he rattled off three or four prominent criminal attorneys in the metro area.

"O.K., thanks. I'll try to call you later." I never did. I couldn't bring myself to do it.

My final phone call was to the Assistant Vice-President of Risk Management, in a feeble effort to salvage something, anything, from my past.

"This is Lynda."

"Lynda, this is Dan Grauer." The tears unleashed once again. "I want to apologize to you. The railroad, a quality company that takes care of its employees, did not deserve what I have done. I just want you to know that I have and will continue to cooperate fully in any manner possible."

Silence.

"Lynda, you know I have put in twenty plus quality years at the railroad. My decision-making regarding this one file has been terrible at best. Please, don't forget the thousands of files I worked hard on and represented the railroad to the best of my ability. Would you consider allowing me to resign?"

"No!" came the immediate answer. She continued to speak, but I had quit listening. For the fourth time this morning, all I seemed to hear was true disappointment and total loss of respect.

I don't even remember hanging up the phone before I felt a hand on my shoulder.

"Dan, I need to escort you off railroad property now. Do you want me to drive you home? Are you going to be all right?" I looked up into yet another set of eyes that revealed only disappointment and sadness. I tried to stand, but was too weak; I fell back into the chair. With a hand under one arm to steady me, I was helped into my coat and was guided toward the elevator. I thought the walk to the auditors' office was long, but that was nothing compared with this. This was the end of a career, the end of a third-generation career.

The quiet, yet firm hand that continued to support me suddenly stopped and turned my body so that we faced one another.

Larry quietly asked, "You wanted to get caught, didn't you?"

"Dan, you have the knowledge, the intelligence, and the authority. What on earth caused you to become so reckless, so careless? I looked at this file and I'll tell you what I think!"

I apparently was going to hear his theory whether I really wanted to or not. . .

"I think that this started out as you trying to take care of a friend and it spiraled out of control. I think that you became obligated in some way, possibly blackmailed into providing ongoing money. I think that when no end was in sight, you decided to become outrageously greedy and sloppy in your handling of the file. I also think that you had a hand in suggesting the audit of this file. How else would a 1996 personal injury file end up on an audit list whose other personal injury files were dated 1999 and 2000?"

"I guess it doesn't make any difference now, does it?" I responded. "It was all still very, very, very wrong!"

During the next ten minutes, I listened to a story about another employee who had defrauded the company in some manner, about how this person hadn't given up on life, actually went on to another career and was quite happy and content. Then nothing else was said.

As we approached my truck a very solemn and quiet voice spoke. "Dan, you're not going to do anything stupid are you?"

"No promises . . . no promises," was the only answer I could give.

I unlocked my truck and slipped in behind the steering wheel. I glanced at my watch; it was only 10:30 a.m. I started my truck and slowly backed out of the parking stall. In many years, I have never driven so slowly exiting the parking garage. As I looked in the rear-view mirror, a lone special agent, and friend, gave a single wave goodbye.

Chapter 5

I remember the day I made the decision to try and right this wrong; it was June 18, 2000 --- Father's Day.

The hustle and bustle of getting ready to go to church had begun. This day would be no different than any other Sunday: a shower, a hot cup of coffee, read the newspaper, and get dressed for church. If anyone remembered it was Father's Day we would eat lunch at a restaurant; somewhere nice, but quick and inexpensive, because like most other Sundays during the summer, a majority of the day would be spent at the Ralston Girls softball complex. During this time of the year, our evenings usually ended at the softball fields somewhere around 10:00 – 10:30 p.m..

I slipped into a khaki pair of Dockers and rust-colored polo shirt. I was tying my shoes and making a futile attempt at keeping our pesky cat out of the way, when I received my first Father's Day greeting.

"Happy Father's Day!" came a somewhat garbled wish.

I looked up and saw feet and legs covered with coffee-tan pantyhose, that also covered a white pair of hip-hugger panties. As my eyes continued upward, I saw an exposed belly, creamy white and fair skinned, a bright white bra covering an ample bosom, and arms that were stretched toward the ceiling.

At the same time, coming downward was a pale-yellow dress that encompassed a summertime pattern of flowers. Somewhere between the exposed tummy and outstretched hands, still behind the fabric of the descending dress, was the source of the greeting.

"Thank you," I laughed, as the dirty blonde hair and pretty face of a woman who looked younger than her years shot through the top of the dress. Her hair was now messed, despite the efforts of styling mousse, a curling iron, and a hair pick.

She walked back toward the mirror and, once again, began adjusting and readjusting the out-of-place hair.

"I suppose we better get the kids up and around," Sara muttered, while trying to apply mascara to one eye.

"I'll get them." I walked to the common area between their rooms. Like a drill sergeant shouting orders, I immediately began a stupid song, at least according to our daughters, but an effective tool in getting them out of bed.

"Rise and shine! Rise and shine! Get your butts out of bed, rise and shine!" I would continue singing and increasing the volume until someone said, "Enough already!"

I laughed and walked to the kitchen for a hot cup of coffee.

I looked at my watch as we left the house; it was 9:50 a.m. The church service at St. Luke United Methodist Church began at 10:15 a.m.; we always seemed to cut it close. Approximately fifteen minutes later, we pulled into the parking lot. The girls jumped out and headed for "Coke discussion," without waiting for mom and dad. This was the typical Sunday morning church entrance for the Grauer family.

Sara walked down the main isle of the sanctuary, about halfway to the front, and turned into the nearest pew on her left. Some things never seem to change; we had sat in this general vicinity of the sanctuary every Sunday for as long as I could remember. I looked around and all the familiar faces were in place, exactly in their spot as if they owned that particular spot of the church.

Something at the front of the sanctuary caught my attention. I looked up, and a light brighter than I ever remembered seeing was coming through the stained-glass window, but as I looked harder, the light was brightest and most illuminating coming through that portion of the window that outlined a huge cross. The glass within the cross was blood red, and yet the light was so intense that it came through as a pure and bright gold color.

I had spent many sleepless nights praying and speaking with God regarding my love of money, my need to "keep up with the Jones'," and my need to feel important both within my family and within society. I also believed that many times in the past six months, He gave me opportunities and choices to end these sins; I had simply chosen not to change.

Why was this feeling so strong in my mind and heart on this particular morning? I had prayed daily for forgiveness of this weakness and guidance in what to do, and, suddenly, I had a feeling an answer was at hand, like it or not.

"Are you O.K.?" I looked to my left and saw concern in the soft hazel eyes staring at me.

"I'm fine, why?"

"Your face is flushed and you're sweating. Are you feeling all right?"

"No," but I wasn't about to offer an explanation. Not yet.

To me, it always seemed as though the first half of the church service went quickly. The invocation, greeting of one another, announcements, a couple of hymns, and we were ready for the sermon. While I don't remember the exact words of the sermon on that day, I do recall in vivid detail what I heard: "On this first Father's Day of the twenty-first century, let us honor our fathers, both living and deceased, for believing in our dreams and helping us to achieve them. Throughout the year, let us continue to reflect on the importance of fathers and pray for their wisdom, guidance, and discernment, whether biological, foster, adoptive, or stepfathers, as role models in our lives. In addition, let us express our gratitude for the many gifts they bring to our lives by passing on their legacy of love and caring to our own children. That through God's grace, mercy, and endless love, we set an example like that set by our Father in Heaven."

My eyes welled with tears and my jaw hung slack. Did this include me? I hadn't fit into this fatherly mold for quite some time. I didn't want my children to follow the example set by their father, especially over the past two years. A thief, a liar, and a fraud was not someone of whom to be proud. I had become an embarrassment and failure as a father, certainly no role model. I closed my eyes and dreamed of a time when I was a good father, a coach, a mentor, and a Christian. What had happened?

"Hey, come back!" I felt a tap on my leg and, once again, looked into concerned eyes.

"I'm fine, really!" I repeated for no less than the fourth time in the last hour.

How could I tell my family? What would the future hold if I simply told the truth, all of it? What choices did I have?

In an attempt to distract my thoughts, I picked up the Bible in our pew, opened it, and randomly began flipping pages as I stared, once again, at the cross, etched into the stained glass. I looked down at the Bible in my lap. It was open to Psalm 16:7 – 8: "I will bless the Lord who counsels me; he gives me wisdom in the night. He tells me what to do, I am always thinking of the Lord, and because he is so near, I never need to stumble or fall." All three of my brothers were devout Christians, and I recall that each of them on separate occasions told me that when God is in control of your life, He will talk to you through His word, the study of the Bible. I was certain each of them had probably read the Bible, front to back, on numerous occasions; I never had. Was God trying to get my attention? Well, let me think about this for just a minute. If I constantly think about the Lord and His way of living, we can apparently gain insight that will help us make good choices and decisions. By communicating with God, He will give us counsel and wisdom.

Suddenly, like a light being turned on by a light switch, I began to both understand and to increase my denial, all at the same time. I quickly looked up and glanced around the church to see if anyone had noticed my embarrassment. Why could I not believe that God would talk to me? My mind began to swirl and negativity set in; I began to validate my failures. God doesn't really work that way; I have prayed for a very long time for an answer to this turmoil, so why now? Who am I that God would take time to provide guidance and direction to a thief, a sinner, and a failure as both a husband and father? I refuse to believe that I am worthy of Him, of His time, and of His love.

I shut the Bible and looked up at the stained-glass window. As I re-entered my own little world of self-pity and fear, the sharp, almost blinding light, reappeared, flowing through the cross in the glass with a renewed intensity.

I prayed. I prayed with all my heart and soul, "Dear Father in Heaven, please, please help me to make the right decisions. I know that what I have done is wrong. How do I make this nightmare stop?" A cold sweat began to form on my forehead; the sweat ran down the back of my neck, underneath my shirt, and down my sides. The church had suddenly become very hot.

The Bible was still in my lap. I glanced to my left to make sure Sara did not notice the anxiety I was feeling. She was watching the choir, her leg moving up and down to the music's rhythm. The awareness of my own surroundings had disappeared. I hadn't heard the music, the prayers, and very few of the words regarding this service.

I opened the Bible, again. I stood it on edge with the binding still touching my lap and let the pages fall open. My eyes were drawn like magnets to Isaiah 30:21: "Whether you turn to the right or to the left, your ears will hear a voice behind you saying, 'This is the way; walk in it.' Then you will defile your idols overlaid with silver and your images covered with gold; you will throw them away . . ."

This simply cannot be happening! This is what books and movies are written about. The cold sweat that had begun a few minutes earlier took off like a leaky water faucet. I looked up at our pastor, still teaching the congregation, then I looked at my watch; what seemed like hours had only been minutes. I was really beginning to get scared now; knowing and believing in the power of God made me extremely nervous, and yet anxious to see what he might have in store.

I looked back to the pulpit. Our pastor was seemingly trying to make a point, and it appeared to me as though he was staring a hole right through me. A hand touched my leg and I jumped as though a firecracker had gone off under the church pew.

"Are you all right?" Sara whispered. "We can leave if you're not feeling well."

"I'm fine, REALLY," grabbing the handkerchief from my back pocket and mopping my forehead. Many people had told me that when you are looking for an answer to a prayer, you must listen with your heart and not just your ears. It dawned on me that maybe I was hearing God for the very first time.

Up until recently, I had always considered myself a Christian, and, yet, when I thought long and hard about my life and how I lived, my life philosophy went directly against the teachings of God. My values and morals seemed seriously out of order. I was going through the motions without the commitment. I thought about Isaiah; when the people of Jerusalem left God's path, He corrected them. Could it really be that God is trying to show me the answer, and given my many human weaknesses, I am missing it? The Bible was full of stories of those who blindly followed God's teachings and were blessed. Could I be one of those people?

I don't recall exactly what happened next, but I remember challenging God to some kind of game. "O.K., God, if you can make it three in a row, I'll try to work with you here and give some serious consideration to having you lead my life again."

I grabbed the Bible one more time. This time I was going to cheat; I was determined not to let the Bible fall open into the Old Testament. I thought that just maybe this all was way too coincidental. I flipped to the New Testament, closed my eyes, and let the Bible fall open.

Again, my eyes were directed toward a specific passage. I focused immediately on James 1:22 – 25: "And remember, it is a message to obey, not just listen to. So, don't fool yourselves. For if a person just listens and doesn't obey, he is like a man looking at his face in a mirror; as soon as he walks away, he can't see himself anymore or remember what he looks like. But if anyone keeps looking steadily into God's law for free men, he will not only remember it but he will do what it says, and God will greatly bless him in everything he does."

This could have been a television commercial. I felt as though I were caught up in the battle often depicted with an angel on one shoulder and the devil on the other: both trying to convince me to follow them, both fighting for control of my mind, body, and soul. Common sense was telling me that it was important to listen to what God's word says, but it was much more important to obey it and to do what the word says. Was I man enough to walk the talk? I had no idea. I quickly scratched down the three Bible passages on the back of a pink, counter-deposit slip from my billfold. I was going to give this some serious consideration.

The ruckus of everyone standing and singing the benediction response brought me back to reality. I couldn't begin to explain what had taken place in the last hour, but I knew in my heart that it was something significant, whatever "it" was. Truly, I don't remember much of the service at all. I glanced over my shoulder as we were waiting in line to leave the sanctuary; the bright golden light was gone from the stained-glass cross. I believed that a challenge had just been laid out before me, and the choice was mine to make. Do I choose to follow God's path or not?

"What is going on?" Sara asked, as we stood waiting to greet the pastor.

"Nothing, I'm fine," I replied, not very convincingly.

The congregation slowly moved to the back of the church where the traditional coffee, donuts, and gossip awaited. A hand on my shoulder stopped me in my tracks.

As I turned, I looked squarely into the eyes of Pastor Craig. Something in his eyes told me that he knew. Impossible! Was God so all-powerful that He would direct others to help me as well? My eyes blurred with tears; without a word, I quickly turned and walked toward the coffee pots, wiping my eyes so that no one else would see. An eerie sense of calm came over me as I sat down and contemplated the last hour. The church coffee was hot, the donuts fresh, and for the first time, in a very long time, I felt a renewed sense of worthiness.

Chapter 6

The drive home from church was extremely quiet; no one said much of anything. I looked into the rear-view mirror; the girls were staring out the side windows from the back seat. Sara was busy looking at some of the church handouts and materials regarding upcoming youth activities, events, and church camps. I was deep in thought and reflection, contemplating how I could act on God's wisdom and advice while not allowing the roof to cave in on myself and my family.

Two obvious chores existed, one much easier than the other. The truth could be potentially devastating; on the other hand, I was confident I could cover-up any wrongdoings and erase all traces of impropriety.

As we pulled into the driveway, a sudden roar rolled from the backseat.

"Happy Father's Day!" the girls yelled in unison.

I had been in such deep thought that the suddenness of their screams just about made me pee my pants. I looked in the rear-view mirror and the girls had tears streaming down their cheeks, they were laughing and giggling so hard. Sara had a smile from ear to ear. I wondered if she was part of this scare tactic.

Tiffany spoke first. "Daddy, since it's Father's Day, can we go out and eat?"

"Are you buying?" I countered. "If it's Father's Day, are you going to make me buy my own lunch"?

"Mom will buy," came the quick response from Alisha.

"Where do we want to go?"

"Valentino's!" came the simultaneous reply from the girls, almost as if they had given it some advanced thought. I looked at Sara and she shrugged her shoulders.

"Well, let's change clothes so that we can go directly to the ball fields when we are done."

The first order of business upon entering the house was to make sure that K.C. was fed and watered and to let the cat into the house from the garage. The girls scampered off to their rooms to change into more comfortable clothes. Sara went to the kitchen to load the dishwasher and get it started before we went out for the day.

I stopped at the entryway to the kitchen and just watched. We had been married for nineteen years; would we make twenty? I prayed a silent prayer, "Lord, if this truly is what you want me to do, please take care of my family as this storm unfolds." Needing to be alone for a few minutes, I retired to the bedroom to change clothes and continue reflecting on the message God had planted in my heart.

I slipped out of my dress pants and shirt, turned, and looked into the dresser mirror. Stress seemed to have escalated the aging process. The bags under my eyes folded right into the wrinkles and lines along the outer edge of my forehead and face. I felt old. I truly did not know the person staring back at me.

What happened to the caring and concern for others? There has always been a part of me that didn't want to grow up. I never wanted to lose the ability to play, to joke around, or just be silly with my kids. I wanted to believe in magic, not falling into the adult trap of only believing what was seen, and yet the kid inside of me was no where to be found. The dreamer had become extinct, the father and husband neglectful.

I used to dream of taking trips with my family, where we were truly connected emotionally and spiritually. The family wholeness and oneness was a priority. When had my dreams turned materialistic? When had I allowed the gold and silver idols to take control?

I again looked at my reflection, concluding I really didn't know where the Dan Grauer of the past had gone. It was painfully obvious that the values and morals with which I had been raised had somehow been buried or, at best, temporarily misplaced. The greater struggle would be answering the question, "Why?" Why did I allow this to happen? The answer was staring me in the face. I had begun to worship money and not

God. Money had taken control of my life. I had become accustomed to living a life style I could not afford.

As I sat on the edge of the bed and looked again at the "man" in the mirror, deep inside, I knew that only one avenue of escape was plausible. It would require that I give up my current life style and give my life totally and unconditionally to God. This avenue would require total honesty, truth, and courage. It might very well destroy not only me, but my family as well. Once again, a sudden calm and peacefulness swept over my body, mind, and soul, like standing near the edge of a crystal, clear lake whose pure blue water seems to reach to the edge of the earth. The trees carried a soft and gentle breeze that touched the wholeness of my body. The lake's edge was painted with an infinite color scheme that enveloped me and magnified the calming effect. The sky, a cloudless baby blue, extended as far as anyone could see in all directions. My decision was made.

Alisha scampered in and jumped on the bed. "Let's go!" She gave me a big hug and kisses on the cheek, then disappeared as quickly as she had appeared.

Father's Day 2000 was without a doubt the hardest and most difficult day mentally, physically, and spiritually that I had lived to date. However, I also knew that given my decision, life was going to get much worse before it got better. Could I do it? Would our family stay intact? Would they understand? How could they ever forgive me?

Chapter 7

I awoke on Monday with a strange enthusiasm. I felt like a very heavy burden had been lifted from my shoulders. This was not going to be easy, but I felt good about the direction in which my life was now pointed.

Arriving at the office, I sat at the computer and immediately began to access every available electronic record and document surrounding the McLloyd personal injury file. Two cups of coffee and a stack of printer paper later, I had compiled a relatively extensive list of payments that had been made from 1996 to present date.

"Vickie!" I hollered out my office door.

"I'm busy, Lieutenant Dan, I don't have time for you today," came the giggling smart-assed response.

"Get in here."

"What do you want?"

"Vickie, please order all the McLloyd files from 1996 to present. There are three of them, numbers 18951, 18954, and 20143. I need all the paperwork, documentation, and records associated with this guy."

"Why? Does he have more expenses? We have paid him a ton, certainly more than he deserves."

I felt the heat in my face; it must have been beet red. I was embarrassed, even Vickie knew! "Why do you say that?"

"I taped all the receipts to the typing paper for you, remember? I saw the trailers, golf cart, and all the crap he really didn't need."

"That's enough, Vickie, you can leave now."

"You're way too nice, Lieutenant Dan. Someday it's going to come and bite you right in the butt! It'll take a couple of weeks; I'll get what you want."

Painstakingly and with an auditor's accuracy, I began to sift through the expenses paid to McLloyd. I detailed legitimate and questionable expenses, medical verses nonmedical, and a final column for ridiculous reimbursements. An in-depth review of the medical records in the files was also undertaken. Did the additional surgeries, medical treatments, prescription costs, and ongoing therapy necessitate the amount of expenses reimbursed? I knew the answer without doing the math: not in a million years. There was absolutely no justification for some of the expenses that had been reimbursed. What in the hell was I thinking?

I stopped typing at the keyboard, laid down my pen, and looked at the complete picture I had painted from the file review. The actual claims settlement was reasonable and in line with other similar personal injury claims settlements, but the expenses had climbed into the hundreds of thousands of dollars, simply unbelievable. I had no supporting documentation, receipts, or the mandatory paperwork needed to make such reimbursements, and yet, I had obviously given thought to how this could be done. A review of the drafts written showed amounts that were just under $10,000; this was my authority limit without anyone reviewing or signing off on the expenditure. As I glanced through the carbon copy drafts, I mentally made note of a total dollar amount paid to McLloyd, without justification. The first of many waves of nausea hit me like a freight train hitting a car at a crossing. The impact was overwhelming, throwing me into a spiral that I seemed to have no control over. My mind immediately began to calculate the "kickback" I had received from McLloyd, and, once again, I was amazed at how uncontrollable the avalanche had gotten.

I had to stop. I organized and compiled all the paperwork and placed it in the black attaché file carrier in my office. I placed the file carrier under my desk. I just couldn't believe what I had seen, what I had done, and, worse yet, what I needed to do. I looked at my watch. It was 3:30 p.m, and I was hungry. Today was intense. I hadn't taken a break, but I needed one badly.

I left my office and walked to the elevator wondering, if I had really received all of that money, where had it all gone? The first floor of our building housed fast-food restaurants and a quick shop. I walked into the quick shop and grabbed a soda and a banana, looking longingly at the beer, but knowing that if I started, I might not stop, given the mood I was in.

Back in my office, I closed my door and stared at the computer screen, not really seeing anything, but thinking about the decision I had made, and the promise I had made to God. Could I really keep my promise? Wouldn't it just be easier to destroy the records and hide the evidence in the black attaché? I knew I had the computer permissions and authorities necessary to destroy any trace of this file, but that would be the easy way out, and that was exactly what had landed me in this position in the first place.

The future was going to be a struggle, a battle between right and wrong, and God's way or the easy way; I wasn't looking forward to it.

I grabbed my keys and left, enough for one day.

Chapter 8

June 2000 to January 2001 was a blur. I don't remember a day that I didn't contemplate my future. I continually played the "what if" game. What if I could find a way to make this go away, without losing it all? What will happen if I just lay it all on the table? What if I just ignore the situation, would it go away?

Part of my job as Senior Manager of Occupational Claims was to interact with the law department and decide which cases we should stand firm on and take to trial, versus those we could potentially settle at an amount that was both win-win for the railroad and the claimant. California had become a litigious nightmare for the railroad, and I was spending an increasing amount of time in Sacramento and the Bay area. The railroad had given our department permission to hire a legal team of attorneys that specialized in occupational claims. Together we had built a defense stable of physicians, defense experts, accident re-constructionists, and ergonomists that was second-to-none in the business world. I truly enjoyed the high-stakes court battles and games; for me it was like a chess game, and my job was to think one step ahead of what my opponent, the claimant, was thinking.

I had gained the respect and trust of our in-house legal department and our outside expert attorneys, as well as the railroad Senior Management. We were beginning to win the war of litigation, one battle at a time. I felt important, wanted, and relied upon. I felt that I was trusted enough to develop, document, and implement critical defense strategies that would, hopefully, have a positive impact on occupational claims in the future of the railroad. I had become so self-confident and egotistical that I began to consider myself invaluable to the railroad, believing that they couldn't possibly do this without me. I was riding a high that I had never felt before in a career, or in my lifetime for that matter.

This attitude carried over into my personal life as well. I can remember putting on the façade of "life couldn't be better" to all those whom I came in contact. I had become a girls softball commissioner in the league where my girls played softball. I was taking my son to debate tournaments throughout the United States, exposing him to the brightest and best competitors. I even went to church every Sunday, sat in the pew with all the other businessmen, and pretended to be the Christian God wanted me to be. Life was grand indeed!

I don't even remember what day it was. I was home on a Saturday morning looking through the mail that had come to the house while I was busy playing hero to the railroad in Sacramento during the previous week, and there it was, a standard nine inch by thirteen inch, manila envelope addressed to Dan Grauer with a return address of L. McLloyd, Little Rock, Arkansas. A lump formed in my throat and I couldn't swallow. In a matter of seconds, my heart began to beat like a tribal drum during a war dance, faster and faster, louder and louder. For a brief moment, I thought I was truly having a heart attack, but came to realize it was anxiety that had taken control of my body. I slowly picked up the envelope and stared. I had not received one of these for many months; I had thought we were done. I was sure there would be no more money demands, reimbursements of nonexistent expenses, or factitious medical treatments. How could I have been so wrong to think that once the snowball had began to grow in size and accelerate down the mountainside, it could stop halfway down the mountain? I was devastated, angry, and overcome with a sense of helplessness.

I slowly opened the envelope and removed its contents, spilling them onto the oval coffee table in front of our sofa. A stack of receipts the size of my fist was wrapped in a poorly handwritten letter. I unwrapped the letter from around the receipts and began to read. "Dear Dan, enclosed is a stack of receipts that are related to my most recent ongoing medical treatment for my shoulders and elbows. When can I expect reimbursement?" I was glad I was already sitting on the couch and that no one else was in the room, because at that moment I was so weak I couldn't have punched my way out of a wet, paper bag. My heart sank and tears welled in my eyes; there would be no easy way out for me. I was certain: this was

God's reminder of a promise I had made months ago and had not yet acted upon. Was I being punished? Would this be the last demand?

"Dan, what are you staring at? Why do you have tears running down your cheeks? What's wrong?" I must have stared at Sara for several minutes, not really seeing her nor comprehending her questions. I felt a hand touch my leg and a voice of concern say, "Well, are you going to talk to me or not?"

I folded the letter and put all of the contents back in the envelope, sealing it once again. "Nothing. Mr. McLloyd is having more medical difficulty and the longer this goes on the more I hate it that a friend is in pain." I hoped she would believe my lie.

"This is certainly an emotional case for you. Are you sure you're O.K.?"

Getting up from the couch and turning so that my back was to Sara, I wiped the tears from my cheeks and quickly pivoted to face her. "Yup, I'm fine. So what's on today's agenda?"

Sara spilled out a list of things to do, items that needed fixed, and kids' activities that would have taken an entire team of laborers to complete in one weekend.

"Well, we better hit the road then." I sighed and walked toward the front door. My mind, however, was in a totally different world. What now? What was plan B?

Chapter 9

It was 10:30 p.m. when we walked back through the front door. The girls were quiet and tired from the days' activities and headed immediately to their rooms. I was certain I wouldn't see them again until I woke them up to get ready for church.

"What a day," Sara moaned as she completed the nightly routine when it was known that we were home for the evening. This routine consisted of kicking off her shoes somewhere around the front door, and by the time she was in the dining room, she was sliding her bra out through the sleeve of her shirt, and scratching her boobs as though it was the greatest feeling in the world. By the time she hit the bedroom, her shorts were down around her ankles and she was headed to the bathroom to pee one last time before getting under the covers. I have to admit, this routine made me smile even after nineteen years.

It was after 11:30 p.m. when I crawled under the covers. Sara was beginning to relax and her eyes were partially closed. Fresh in my mind was the manila envelope I'd received in the mail and what it meant for my career, my life, and my family. I knew this was going to be a sleepless night, so I reached for my headphones in hopes that some music would help take my mind away from the horrible future I was envisioning. Had I known what was going to happen next, I most certainly would have turned on the TV instead. As I settled back into my pillow and ensured the headphones were snug against my ears, a song on the radio pulled hard at the strings attached to my heart. As I listened, I turned toward my wife, wondering exactly if the words I was hearing would ring true as Garth Brooks sang:

Sometimes late at night,
I lie awake and watch her sleeping.
She's lost in peaceful dreams,
So I turn out the lights and lay there in the dark.
And the thought crosses my mind,
If I never wake up in the morning,
Would she ever doubt the way I feel
About her in my heart?

If tomorrow never comes,
Will she know how much I loved her?
Did I try in every way to show her every day
That she's my only one?
And if my time on earth were through,
And she must face the world without me,
Is the love I gave her in the past
Gonna be enough to last
If tomorrow never comes?

Another option crept into my mind: what if tomorrow never came? Would that make things go away? Would it be better for my family, or was that just another easy way out? I thought about my promise to God and dismissed any other resolution, at least for now. However, as I lay awake putting together scenario after scenario, it bothered me that I had even remotely considered suicide. I prayed that thought would never again enter my mind. I remember looking at the clock at 4:17 a.m., and the next thing I knew the alarm was going off at 8:30 a.m., getting us up for church. As I sat up in bed rubbing my eyes, trying to make sense of all my thoughts during the last eight hours, I realized this was only one of many, many long days to come.

Monday morning came way too early, and the weekend was much too short. I had concluded that I needed to call Mr. McLloyd and see if we could put a stop to this nonsense, but a real part of me was terrified. I couldn't seem to identify where the terror was coming from, whether it was from all that had taken place in the past, or whether it came with fear of the future. I had arrived at my office unusually early for two reasons:

first, to call McLloyd, and second, to avoid the jovial Vickie. I just wasn't in the mood.

I picked up the phone and dialed. Lance answered on the second ring.

"McLloyd residence."

"Lance, this is Dan. How are you doing?"

"Hey, Dan. Nothing ever seems to change much. I am enjoying retirement, fishing, and the grandkids. I hate the ongoing shoulder, elbow, and neck problems. It never seems to end. Did you send money for that last set of receipts I sent to you?"

"That's what I am calling to talk to you about. I can't keep on doing this. My life is headed to the shitter emotionally, and we just need to stop."

Silence. . .

"Well, the way I see this is that you're taking care of ongoing problems, and because you're taking care of me, I'm taking care of you. Nobody can tell me what to do with my money, and if I see fit to send some to you, then so be it. I really need this money to keep going. I can't do all the things I used to because of what the railroad did to me. We have been friends for a long time, you have been down to my place, and we have gone out on the lake. I'm taking care of you too! I really need you to do this for me."

"I don't know if I can, Lance."

"Dan, I can't raise my arms above my shoulders. I can't work around the house or do any of the maintenance anymore. The railroad took away my life. Don't you do the same thing."

"I appreciate everything you have done for me, Lance, but part of what's happening to you is old age. Given the number of surgeries and problems, arthritis has to be an issue for you. When does it stop?"

"Damn it, Dan. Your family has been able to do things and buy things you wouldn't normally have been able to afford or do. You still owe me. You really NEED to help me here."

I don't know whether or not at that point in time I finally came to realize that there would be no end to this milking of money, but what I heard was that there would be consequences if I didn't continue. I knew this had to come to an abrupt end. Maybe I was reading too much into this conversation, but then again, maybe not!

"Fine, you'll have your money shortly," and I hung up the phone.

Lance, ole' boy, you want to play games — well, then let the games begin. I knew immediately what I was going to do. I had given a good deal of thought to a plan that I would use only if these very circumstances happened in the exact order in which they just took place. I would send Lance his money all right, plus more money and more money and more money. If I was going down, McLloyd was coming with me. I knew my authority to reimburse expenses was $10,000. McLloyd was going to get checks every two weeks, receipts or no receipts, and, come hell or high water, this crap was going to end.

I opened my office door and hollered, "Vickie! Come in here, please!"

"Hey, Lieutenant Dan, how was your weekend? What do you need?"

"Here is another stack of receipts from McLloyd. I need to send another reimbursement check to him. Would you tape them to paper for me?"

"No."

"Excuse me?"

"I said, NO! Are you hard of hearing?"

I paused for a moment and looked hard into Vickie's eyes. She knew, she had to, and once again she was right, I needed to protect her and if this was going down as I anticipated, Vickie did not need to be involved.

"Don't do it, Lieutenant Dan."

"You can leave now, Vickie."

She turned and walked away without another word, without another word for the remainder of the day as I recall.

I got up and closed the door to my office, again. I needed to keep this plan concealed and completely separate from any other work I was doing. I was going to document everything and put it in the black attaché telling the entire story of fraud and kickbacks, because when the time came and all was revealed, I wanted no doubt left in anyone's mind as to who was guilty besides Dan Grauer.

I don't remember how many drafts for reimbursement were sent to McLloyd over the next few months. I knew that I had implemented and engaged in a plan that would expose it all, and yet, at the same time, destroy a career, a livelihood, and possibly a family. On two occasions, I took the black attaché home, with every intention of destroying its contents and wiping away all traces of the atrocity, and on two occasions, I brought the black attaché back to its resting place under my desk.

In October 2000, I don't remember the exact day, but I remember reading the e-mail. In the fourth quarter of each year, the auditors would look at those claims settled in the previous year and throughout the current year as a system of checks and balances for those of us that were entrusted with appropriation of company funds for personal injury claims. Could this be the opportunity to finally bring closure to years of anxiety and frustration? How could I use this event as a means to bring the past to the forefront?

I grabbed my notebook and headed toward the boss's office. I told Ron that this particular case was dragging on forever and I needed some guidance in getting it brought to resolution. We spent the next thirty minutes reviewing all the notes and documentation electronically. Ron made mention several times that McLloyd sure had been reimbursed a great deal of money over and above the claims settlement, " . . . especially in the last few months." I admitted that this is one file that I felt got totally out of control and I certainly did not handle it as well as I should have.

"Give me a day to review everything and we'll talk again, Dan."

"No problem."

My heart was beating so intensely that I felt sure I would faint the minute I stood up to leave. I knew Ron well enough to know that this was only the beginning of his investigation into this file, and I had a gut feeling as to what the anticipated outcome would be.

The next morning all my thoughts were validated. An updated list had been sent out regarding the files to be reviewed by the audit team and at the top of the list was McLloyd's claim. Just as I was reading the e-mail, my phone rang.

"Dan, this is Ron. Can you come over to my office to discuss the McLloyd file?"

"Sure, I'll be there in just a minute."

I walked slowly to the office of my boss. I remember thinking I was going to be immediately fired and escorted out of the building. All I could think of was my family and of all things, the fact that Christmas was coming up!

"Hey, Dan, have a seat. I have spent several hours reviewing the McLloyd file. Is there anything you want to tell me?"

Here it was. My chance to air all the dirty laundry, do the right thing, and yet I was too scared. Although I couldn't look Ron in the eyes, I did manage a meager, "No, why do you ask?"

"This case just seems very unusual in comparison to the thousands of other claims you have handled. Are you sure there's nothing you want to tell me?"

"No, nothing I can think of right now anyway."

I could only hope my lies were good enough to get me back out the door and back to my office.

"O.K., that'll be all."

I don't ever recall almost running out of Ron's office as I did on this particular occasion, embarrassed and ashamed. Back in my office, I sat down with my elbows on my desk, my face in my hands, and I wept. My career would end soon. Was this the right thing to do? How could I have done this to my family? What would the future hold? God, it's in your hands now!

Each and every day following, I lived in fear. The auditors would be looking at files from November through February, and I knew that when they looked at the McLloyd file, my career was over. I had lost interest in California litigation, in the development of strategic defense planning, helping injured employees return to a sense of wholeness, and of all I had once loved about my job at the railroad. I stopped going out with friends and attended church sporadically. I withdrew into a world of daily battles with my psyche: right versus wrong, materialism and money versus quality of life, family first versus God first, and responsibility, blame, and mere survival.

I couldn't bring myself to tell my family. It was coming up on Christmas and everyone was excited. I would try to make this a Christmas to remember for my family because it might be the last in a long while. I couldn't comprehend how they would feel when their father and provider would go from a salary of $75,000 per year to nothing, and possibly to jail. What would Sara do? We had become complacent in a life style of beyond necessity, into a world of new furniture, cars, a newly remodeled home, and travel. We lived on credit cards and wants. Our world as we knew it was about to come crashing down, hard! What about mom and dad? How do I tell them that greed had ended the third, and most likely the last, generation working at the railroad? What would I say? When should I tell them?

Physically, the stress was taking a toll. Nausea overwhelmed me on a daily basis, frequent headaches, and body aches dramatically increased. I took more sick time and vacation from November 2000 to January 2001 than I had at any other time in my entire career. Eating was on opposite ends of the spectrum; either I didn't eat at all or I gorged and inhaled everything in sight. It seemed as though I was determined to punish myself in some manner.

Thanksgiving came and went, Christmas came and went, and still, no word from the audit team. I returned to work January 2, just as nervous and unfocused as I had been prior to Christmas. The black attaché was still sitting in its proper spot under my desk. I would spend hours staring at the case, wishing that I could go back and relive the last three years of my life. The reality of the consequences of my actions had begun to take hold, and I was just plain scared.

Finally, on January 11, I was notified that a review of my files was going to begin. I couldn't bear to look at Vickie; our daily interaction was minimal and nonpersonal. At home, I had become a recluse, spending hours on the computer or working on projects that had been left undone. I don't know why, but on Saturday, January 13, I drove to my office, I can't remember the reason or the lie I told Sara. I took what I knew would be a final look around my office, reflecting on my accomplishments and failures. The black attaché was nowhere to be found; this was the beginning of the end.

Chapter 10

I couldn't change the past and what the future held I had no idea, but what about today? I had been fired; now what? The drive home was just as long as the drive in on January 15. I knew that Sara would be coming home for lunch and I need to sit down and talk with her. I had better contact a criminal defense attorney based on what I had been told during the meeting with the auditors. I also needed to tell my family.

I arrived at home around 11:00 a.m. I stepped out of my truck and just stood looking at the outside of the home we had worked on over the past five years, making it just the way we wanted it. The physical and emotional investment had been massive. Both the exterior and interior had been completely remodeled, and the value had almost certainly doubled. Just how much would we lose? I had no idea, but I also knew that we had to get over one hurdle at a time.

Once inside the house, my whole world began to crash. I threw my briefcase on the couch and suddenly found that I couldn't move, as though my feet were buried in concrete. The next thing I remember is hearing a car door shut in the driveway. Sara must be home for lunch.

I found myself on my knees in the entryway of our home. I don't know how long I had been there. I looked at my watch, and it was approaching noon. Had I passed out or did I have a temporary mental breakdown? I knew that I didn't want Sara to find me like this, so I quickly got up off the floor and walked rapidly to the bathroom. I needed to splash some cold water on my face and refocus.

I turned to see Sara's face watching me in the bathroom mirror.

"Are you all right?"

"Is it possible to be both relieved and terrified at the same time?"

"Dan, let's go out to the dining room table and sit down"

I followed Sara down the hallway, but not directly to the table. I had to have some water; my throat felt like a desert. I will never forget the first question Sara asked when I joined her at the table.

"Are you going to hire an attorney?"

It was already beginning. Without having spoken a word, the barrier was being built in our relationship. "Are YOU going to hire an attorney?"---not "WE" but "YOU." I could see this was going to be my issue to deal with, not ours. My heart sank.

"What are YOU going to tell the kids? What are YOU going to tell your family? How are the bills going to get paid?"

"Sara, slow down! Let me answer one question at a time."

Sara hands went to her face and she began to cry. I remember thinking that if I had a hole to crawl into, this would have been the perfect time to do it and pull the world over the top of the hole.

"Sara, listen to me. I talked with Tony before I left. He gave me some names of very good criminal defense attorneys, and I will call them this afternoon. I will talk with the kids right after school, and call my family this afternoon as well. As for money, I will be able to draw unemployment, and there is $50,000 in my 401(k) that we can live on if necessary. I just couldn't keep living the lie, Sara. Didn't you suspect anything when I received checks in the mail from McLloyd?"

"I asked you about it one time and you told me that you were reimbursing claims expenses and that Lance appreciated your help and was trying to help us in return."

"Well, that part was true. Don't you remember the very first check we received?"

"I remember that you sent it back saying that we couldn't accept such a gift. I also remember that we had become financially overwhelmed moving into Omaha and walking into the mess during the closing of our home. I remember that we cashed a check and immediately began to fix all the unseen damage in our home."

"That's right, but didn't you suspect anything when the checks just kept coming?"

"Maybe, but I also knew that the extra money allowed us to do the things we had always wanted. We gave our kids all the things we didn't have growing up. Why didn't you tell me?"

"I guess I saw you happy for the first time in a long, long time. You had always talked about how poor your family was growing up and how hard it was for you. I knew that money was important, and I wanted to give you and the kids all the things I saw my brothers giving their families. I know this sounds stupid, but I guess it became kind of a competition for me to be able to keep up with Dave and Doug. Dave graduated from pharmacy school, got his master's degree and his law degree, and he has become an extremely successful attorney. Doug is an engineer in charge of a pipeline through Kansas and Nebraska. Both of them were very athletic and successful all through high school; they made mom and dad very proud. I wasn't like them; I was different. I wasn't the athlete they were; I liked music and golf.

"I was average at best. I remember all the high school teachers telling me, 'Dan, you sure aren't like your brothers.' Well, guess what? I am not my brothers! I thought that when I got to college it would be different, but I ended up with a professor who had taught Dave, and do you want to know what his first words were? 'Dan, you're sure not like your older brother.' I am and always will be the black sheep of the family. Dennis is exceeding what I see as the 'family expectations.' He was quarterback for a high school football team that almost won the state title. He is working toward his doctorate in pharmaceutical research. Then there is Dan...."

"How long do you think we will be able to keep the house? We took a second mortgage out last year, you have new truck, and our credit cards are at their maximum. Just what are you going to do for income?"

"Sara, can't you see this is about more than money and stuff? I certainly can't condone my decision-making, but it wasn't just me that spent all the extra money."

"I don't want to talk about it now; I have to go back to work so that one of us has some income."

Realization had set in. I was going to be the beating post for what was about to rain down around my family. There was no "us" or "we" in this comedy of errors, and rightfully so, I guess.

After Sara had left, I walked down to my briefcase and pulled out the notes where I had written the names of criminal defense attorneys recommended by Tony. I should really have explained to Tony the situation instead of putting him on the spot, although I am sure, by now, he knew the reason for my phone call. I picked up the phone and dialed.

"Good afternoon. Stallhaber Law Office. May I help you?"

"Yes. Hi, my name is Dan Grauer. I was given Allen Stallhaber's name by a friend of his and I believe I am in a situation where I am in real need of his assistance."

"Hang on, I will transfer you to his office."

"This is Allen Stallhaber. May I help you?"

"Allen, this is Dan Grauer. I work closely with Tony Hadley in the legal department at the railroad and he gave me your name. I am in a situation where I really need your assistance. . ." Some fifteen minutes later I had an appointment to see Allen the next day.

The next series of phone calls would be the most difficult conversations of my life. It was time to tell my family. I called my little brother, Dennis, first. As I dialed the phone, I wondered if I would be able to share the entire ordeal, truthfully and fully.

"This is Dennis."

"Dennis, Dan. Do you have a few minutes to talk?"

"Yea, what's up?"

"Dennis, there is no easy way for me to say this. I was fired this morning."

"What? Really? What happened?"

I began to try to explain, but was overcome with emotion. A huge lump filled my throat and I couldn't talk, because if I did, a river of tears would flow. I bit my lower lip in an attempt to regain composure.

"Dan, are you O.K.?"

It was too late; the flood unleashed and I began to sob. I felt like a child crying so hard. I couldn't get my breath between sobs, nor could I talk without gasping for air between sobs as though it were my last. Dennis was on the other end of the phone and only knew that my railroad career had ended. I know that I tried to explain, but what words were exchanged I had no clue. I don't know how long I stayed on the phone with Dennis. I only vaguely remember his last words. "Dan, you will be in our prayers. Dan, promise me you won't do anything stupid. You need to call your pastor and talk with him. I'll call Dave and Doug and tell them. Can I tell Shar? Please, let me know if there is anything I can do."

Wow! If telling Dennis was that emotionally difficult, how in the world will I be able to tell mom and dad? I waited another thirty minutes, trying to regain my composure and put together the conversation in my head based on how I thought my parents would react. Mom had a stroke several years back; along with the physical complications, several mental side effects took hold as well. As a result, Mom says what she thinks, and her emotions are pretty much worn on the edge of her sleeve, crying and becoming upset with only the slightest provocation.

I looked in the bathroom mirror and was shocked at the man staring back at me. The red, swollen eyes, puffy cheeks, the dark circles under the eyes, and cracked lips were not indicative of the father and husband of the past nineteen years. I shut the light off and walked away, feeling as bad inside as I knew I looked on the outside. Once again, I picked up the phone.

"Hello?"

"Hi, Mom. This is Dan."

"How are you doing, Dan?"

"Not so good, Mom."

"What's wrong?"

I truly would have believed that the human body can cry only a limited number of tears, but I was wrong. It was a repeat performance. Through the tears, the difficulty breathing, the runny nose, and sniffles, I managed to tell mom that I had been fired from the railroad. I offered no explanation and none was asked for. My heart literally broke in two as I heard my mother, through tears of her own, tell me that I need to tell dad, because she couldn't hear any more.

I could hear my mother crying, which was almost more than I could bear. Then I heard dad ask mom, "What's wrong?"

Finally, I heard, "Hello?"

"Hey, Dad. It's Dan."

"What's wrong?"

"Dad, I am so sorry!"

"Sorry for what son?"

How could I tell my father, a man well-respected and dedicated to railroad life, that his son had just ended the third generation of employment with the railroad and in the process tarnished our family's name with what was to come?

"Dad, I was fired today."

As I tried to explain all that had taken place, I could hear dad's breathing become increasingly labored and he became extremely quiet. You see, my father was a big man, standing 6'2" in his socks and weighing a solid 230 pounds. Dad was mostly muscle; I had witnessed my father lifting parts from railroad cars that normally would require mechanical assistance to lift. If he wanted to, his grip could bring most men to their knees.

I had seen my dad cry only one time in the past, the day he accidentally ran over our dog, Pepper, while backing the car out of the garage. Peppy had been a part of the family for many years and, due to loss of hearing, ran right out behind dad as he moved the car, Dad was devastated.

This was to be the second time, and I had caused it. I could hear the hurt and disappointment as dad tried to respond through the lump in his throat that had become painfully noticeable. Dad tried really hard to be supportive, but I had to end the conversation because neither of us could say anything.

"Dad, I'll call later," I said as I hung up the phone.

My mind began to race with all that the future might hold. What in God's name had I done?

Chapter 11

I was going to be sick. I ran down the hall and to the bathroom. I was glad the toilet seat was up or there would have been a mess; however, I was unprepared for what happened next. As I began to vomit, I saw blood clots spray the inside of the toilet along with my stomach contents of the past six hours. Given all that had happened and my continuous deep stomach pain, I wasn't surprised, but what could I do about it now? I had no insurance.

I am sure what seemed like an eternity was only a few minutes. I had really bad shakes and the cold sweats. I remember struggling to make it to the couch. I would stay there until the kids got home.

Ryan, my oldest child, was the first one home; this was his senior year in high school. I was extremely proud of him, as I was of all of my children. He had worked his way into the top five of his class, and ranked nationally in the top fifty debaters. He had worked hard and had the opportunity to attend debate tournaments around the United States. Ryan was going to be attending the University of Chicago, or had I screwed that up as well?

"Dad, what are you doing at home?"

Not wanting to ride the emotional roller coaster three more times, I merely replied, "I am not feeling good and just need to rest for a little bit," which was partially true.

Tiffany came walking through the door next. Tiffany was a freshman in high school and a cheerleader. I never could figure out why she and Ryan couldn't ride home together, but unless there was bad weather, Tiffany always walked. Between athletics and cheerleading, she always seemed to have somewhere to be and something to do.

Alisha was the last one home. Alisha went to grade school just down the hill from our back yard. Alisha was at the tomboy stage of her life where boys, make up, and dresses were nerdy. If you listened you could usually hear Alisha before you saw her walking in the door, laughing, talking with a neighbor friend, or just singing.

After having to tell the girls the same explanation I had told Ryan about being home, everyone started making their routine bathroom stops and putting their book bags in their rooms. I called a family conference. Ryan sat on the love seat perpendicular to the couch; the girls, sharing the couch, sat on each side of me.

"Kids, I've got something to tell you; it's something I am not proud of, and will have a major impact on this family."

I had gotten their attention. Each of them was looking into my eyes wondering what type of hammer was about to drop.

"I was fired today from my job at the railroad."

Silence. . .

Looking at the floor, Ryan was the first to ask, "Why, Dad?"

"Well, this isn't going to be easy to say, but basically I accepted money from a claimant that I didn't deserve. We have been using the money to fix up the house and buy a whole lot of things we really didn't need." For the next thirty minutes, I did the best I could at explaining what had taken place over the past two years.

Tiffany had a look of sheer panic on her face and asked, "Dad, are you going to go to jail?"

"I don't know; I will be meeting with an attorney tomorrow to strategize what is best for me at this point. You need to know, however, that this will most likely make the news. You will hear your teachers and friends talk about what I have done. Parents will talk to their children about what I have done. I wanted you to hear it from me before anyone else told you, or you saw it on the news. This isn't going to be easy for you in the coming weeks. This will be a time when you'll find out who your true friends are and are not."

I looked at Alisha and saw one big, crocodile tear running down her cheek. She threw her hands around my neck, gave me a big hug, and asked the one question I had been asking myself for a very long time but had no answer, "Daddy, why did you do that?"

What could I say? I was brought up by parents with good moral values; they taught me right from wrong. I had a college education and had worked my way into management within the railroad. I had absolutely no clue how to answer her.

"I really don't know, honey!"

We talked for another hour or so about what to expect from what I had done, and how I anticipated this monstrosity would affect their lives. During our conversation, it had become painfully obvious that I had not done a good job of communicating with my children. For the first time in a very long time, I looked deep into eyes that could not cover up the let down, the agony, and the wounds that I had opened in their lives. Yet, they each gave me a long and tight hug, letting me know that no matter what the outcome, they loved me. What kind of father does this to his children?

Sara had arrived home and went immediately to the kitchen. She laid her planner and purse on the kitchen bar and began making dinner. She was facing the stove, browning some hamburger, for what I didn't know. I slowly walked up behind her and hugged her tightly; I could feel the tension as her muscles drew tight and she pulled away. I told her of my conversations with my family and of my appointment with an attorney for tomorrow.

"Sara, I would really like it if you could go to the attorney with me."

"I don't think I can get off work."

"It would mean a lot to me to have you there."

"I told you, I don't think I can get off work."

"O.K. . . . I am so sorry this is happening. I didn't mean this to come down as it has. Sara, I need to tell you, just as I have the kids, this will probably be all over the news, both TV and newspaper. You're going to need to prepare for what your colleagues, friends, and family will say."

"Just what do I tell them, Dan?"

"The truth! You tell them I screwed up. You tell them that greed and selfishness got the best of me, that money became my number one priority instead of God and family."

Sara leaned against me and began to weep. I held her tight and did my best to comfort her and tell her that we would be all right, that God would not let us down, but at the same time, we had a very difficult future ahead of us. Sara's arms continued to hang at her side; the tighter I held her, the less responsive she became. I truly hoped this wasn't a sign of how our future was going to be.

I spent the remainder of the evening by myself, in the living room of our home, watching television. My mind, however, was fixated on the future: What will tomorrow hold? What about a month from now, or a year from now? I had begun to mentally prepare for the worst.

I had hoped and prayed that by telling the truth and trying to make right all that I had done wrong, acceptable sleep patterns would return; however, I had no such luck. As I walked into the bedroom, the television was on; Sara was in bed lying on her back watching the current news story. I undressed while watching the TV and crawled under the covers. Sara promptly turned her back toward me and pretended to go to sleep, no usual cuddling, hug, or good night kiss. I didn't hear the words that I longed for without asking. I needed to know that she would be there, that she would love me, and be by my side through what was to come, but no such words were spoken, nor were they ever from that point forward.

Sara had every right to be angry, as did my children. They had become as much a victim of what I had done as the railroad. As I lay with my hands behind my head, I began to comprehend the breadth of my blunder, the people, emotions, and life styles that were going to be impacted. My stomach began hurt terribly; I turned on my left side, with my back to Sara, and brought my legs up into a fetal position in a feeble attempt to alleviate the pain. This was going to be another long night.

I don't know what time I drifted off to sleep; the TV had come on as usual at 6:00 a.m. Sara was already up and in the shower. I had no idea what to do. My meeting with the attorney was not until 10:30 a.m.; I had nowhere to go. I looked from where I lay in bed through the open bathroom door and watched Sara shower through the frosted shower doors. I felt helpless and weak. What could I say? Was this the right decision?

I got up and helped get the kids ready for school. Sara dressed and left for work without saying a word. I knew that we were going to have to talk and lay all our emotions on the table, work through them one at a time, and decide if we could continue into a twentieth year of marriage. I made a mental note to call our pastor this week and seek some help.

The drive to the attorney's office felt extremely awkward, maybe because the office of Allen Stallhaber was located within two blocks of my now former office. I arrived at approximately 10:15 a.m., anticipating the need to complete an onslaught of paperwork. I was right. A very pleasant, young receptionist sat behind the desk in the outer office. She was on the phone. Catching my glance she held up one finger, indicating she would be with me in a minute as she finished her phone call.

"May I help you?"

"My name is Dan Grauer. I have a 10:30 a.m. appointment with Mr. Stallhaber."

"Have you been here before, Mr. Grauer?"

"No, Ma'am. This certainly is a first for me, and a last for that matter."

Not knowing what I meant, she merely shrugged her shoulders and handed me a clipboard full of documents to complete.

"Mr. Grauer, if you'll complete these as thoroughly as possible, I will let Mr. Stallhaber know you are here."

"Thank you," I said as I sat down and pulled a pen from my shirt pocket. The stack of papers, for the most part, was directed toward collecting personal history. One document that caught my attention was the financial obligation requirements of the law office. As I stared at the document wondering how I could afford this type of defense, I heard, "Mr. Grauer, my name is Allen Stallhaber."

I looked up to see an obviously expensive, three-piece, brown suit. Inside the suit was a man about 5'9" tall, approximately 180 pounds, with a face that had been hardened by years of tough legal defense work for those that were indeed guilty, and those that claimed total innocence. Allen was in his late forties, and balding with hair around the sides and back, and completely bald on top. He presented himself with what I believed to be a genuine smile and a firm handshake.

"Dan, I am in between court hearings so I am limited on time. Come on back."

As he turned to walk away, I saw a ponytail that took me totally by surprise and, at the same time, brought this elegant, legal professional down to a level that made me much more comfortable, at least as comfortable as I could be with the nature of this type of visit. We walked down the hallway, turned to the left, and then proceeded through a small conference area that appeared to be an extension of Allen's office. I was directed to have a chair in front of a dark, cherry, wood desk fitting, in my opinion, for a successful attorney. A quick glance around at the surroundings revealed a moderate décor, not extravagant by any means, but erring on the side of conservative versus lavish.

"Dan, I need you to give me a little more in-depth summary of the current situation than the quick and dirty during our phone conversation of yesterday."

For the next fifteen to twenty minutes, I described for Allen what had taken place over the past two years: what I had done, who was involved, where any illegal monies had been mailed, and how the snowball managed to cascade into a full avalanche of trouble. Allen took copious notes, and at times would spend minutes looking deep into my eyes, almost as if attempting to gauge my honesty. At the end of my synopsis, I found myself with a Kleenex in my hand, once again wiping away the tears, looking across the desk into a face that showed real concern and what I interpreted to be a look of worry.

"Dan, I wish you would have come to me a year ago," Allen said, shaking his head and glancing down at his notes. "I need you to sign some authorizations so that I can get all records related to what you have told me. Do you know if the railroad has turned this over to the U.S. Prosecutor as yet?"

"I don't know, but I don't think so."

"Dan, I do have some really close friends within the railroad law department. I will do everything I can for you, but here's what you can expect, and what I need you to do. First, in the Federal court things move very, very slowly. It could be as much as two years before disposition comes in this case. Second, you need to get a job. Don't lie around the house and do nothing because that will only make it worse. Third, based on your emotional status, you need to get some counseling, whether through your church or professionally. Fourth as difficult as this is, you need to carry on with your life as much as possible. Last, I will always tell you both the worst-case scenario and the best-case scenario. I will tell you to always expect the worst; that way, if it happens you are prepared, if not, then you're all the better. Let's set an appointment up for two weeks from today. That will give me time to do some investigation and collect information. Here is my card. Feel free to call me with any questions or concerns. Now, do you have any questions?"

"Allen, I can only make monthly payments to you. Can you give me an idea what we might be looking at financially?"

"I am going to give you an estimate, but you cannot hold me to this because circumstances change quickly in the litigation arena. If we don't go to trial, can minimize the damages, and my involvement, you will be looking at a minimum of $15,000 to $20,000. If we go to trial, you can expect $30,000 to $45,000. Do you have access to this kind of money or family that can help you?"

"Well, I have my entire 401(k) that I could access with penalty. I know its worth over $50,000, and I will call my family and talk with them."

"You will need to write a $500 check today so that we can get started."

"O.K."

"One more thing, Dan. I want to meet your wife. She is going to need to support you through this entire ordeal. She also needs to know what to expect, and sometimes it helps if I tell her rather than you. Can she come to the next meeting?"

"I'll talk with her and see."

I left the meeting with confidence that I had retained someone who knew the law, would work hard for what was best for his client, and, most importantly, that seemed to care. My full-time job now became to find a job and attempt to move forward with being the husband and provider I needed to be.

Chapter 12

The next two weeks were a flurry of phone calls, computer research, resume updates, and job application mailings. The number one priority was the family finances and looking at how we could make ends meet over the next several months. I contacted my 401(k) representatives, and explained the situation; with some hesitation, I was told that I could withdrawal my portion of the 401(k) under a hardship clause, but would pay a 20 percent penalty for doing so. I asked that the paperwork be mailed to our home.

I called the Railroad Retirement Board, made inquires about drawing unemployment, and began the paperwork process knowing full well that I had to be off a minimum of two continuous weeks before any payment would be considered.

I developed an Excel spreadsheet, outlining all potential income versus payments that needed to be made and areas of our life style that would need drastic trimming. Based on all I had put together, I felt that we could maintain for six to eight months without looking at other extreme options.

Finally, I put together what I felt was a good resume, reference sheet, and job application data that could be utilized in securing new employment. I felt as though we were going to survive.

Sara and I went to another meeting with the attorney. Allen reviewed our previous meeting notes, and began asking Sara some questions.

"Sara, did you know what was going on?"

"Well, Dan said that he was reimbursing expenses to a claimant and that what that claimant does with his money is his business. So, I guess I trusted Dan."

"Didn't you think something was up when all this extra money came rolling in?"

"Yes, but Dan kept telling me it was up to McLloyd to do whatever he wanted with his money."

"Did you ever deposit any of the money and did you help spend the money?"

"Yes. Why?"

"Well, the potential exists that not only will Dan be prosecuted, but if there is any indication that you knew what was going on, you may also be prosecuted."

I stood up and looked at Allen. "Allen, that cannot happen. I will take full responsibility for what has taken place here. I cannot let my children lose both their mother and father due to my stupidity."

"Dan, sit down. I am not going to let that happen, but I want you to be prepared for the worst, remember? Now, it's your turn. Dan, do you have any idea how much money over the past two years you received from McLloyd?"

"No sir, but I'm betting you're going to tell me."

"The railroad is claiming that you received $254,000 over the two-year period and McLloyd received over $500,000 in fraudulent money."

"Horseshit! The money he received regarding personal injury claims was based on wage loss for eleven surgeries he underwent on his shoulders, elbows, and hands. When the settlements were made, they were signed off on by my boss."

"Dan, calm down. I am merely telling you what the railroad is claiming. You see, the railroad has an insurance policy that will reimburse them for any fraudulent monies paid to anyone by someone that represents the company. The more they can claim, the more they will be reimbursed. The downside is that they will do everything they can to prove that the entire personal injury settlement was wrong. Additionally, you need to know that if they are successful, the insurance company will most likely file a civil litigation suit against you. Now don't panic, these are all just possibilities. I am trying to make you aware of EVERYTHING."

"Great, so what's next?"

"Based on my investigation to date and based on what you have told me, I suggest we work with both the railroad and the U.S. Prosecutor to make the best deal we can. The U.S. Prosecutor has not filed any charges as of yet, and I will contact them to see if we can do it in a manner wherein you will not be embarrassed in front of your family. It may take several weeks for the charges to be filed. I will keep you informed and try to stay one step ahead of the prosecution."

"So, what do we do in the mean time?"

"Continue to work toward gaining employment. Pay off as many bills as you can, but most of all, don't give up. Sara, this isn't going to be easy, and if you think Dan is worth fighting for, you need to show that. I am going to do the very best that I can. Do you have any questions?"

"Yes. You said that you always will give worst-case scenario. What is the worst-case scenario for Dan?"

"The Federal sentencing guidelines are based on a point system. I have calculated that the worst-case scenario would be Dan could serve three to five years in a Federal prison facility. The best-case scenario could be probation. The most likely scenario will be somewhere in between these two."

Sara fell quiet and looked at the floor; I could tell she was overwhelmed. I thanked Allen and asked that he call me with any updates of information. This would be the one and only appointment with "my" attorney that Sara ever attended throughout the next twenty-four months.

I was scared. Over the past two to three years, despite having money, it seemed as though Sara and I had grown apart in almost every aspect of our relationship. Was this going to be the "straw that broke the camel's back?" This was one hell of a way to learn that money doesn't equal happiness.

The drive home was extremely quiet. Sara looked out the window of the passenger side of our vehicle the entire trip. I wished that I could have read her thoughts so that we could have talked about all the concerns, the anger, and the build-up of emotion. It was not to be, and this became the beginning of a communication shutdown in our relationship.

As we pulled into our driveway, I looked at Sara, saying, "Sara, we have to talk. I can't read your mind. I understand you're angry and frustrated. I understand you are disappointed. We really need to talk."

"Where did it all go?"

"Where did all of what go?"

"The money. Where did it all go?"

"Well, off the top of my head, about $30,000 went toward remodeling our home, following one of the biggest mistakes of our lives in closing on a home with so many problems. We took a ten-day Hawaiian vacation, took the family to Orlando, drive a newer vehicle, and have a boat and a camper. Our kids have been on European trips and around the United States on various class trips. We have new furniture in the house. Want me to keep going?"

I think that if looks could kill, I would have been dead. Sara stared a hole right through me, and then quickly looked away. She got out of the vehicle, got into her vehicle, and drove away without another word.

As I watched her drive away, I contemplated what had been discussed throughout the morning; it was true that this boiled down to a huge error in judgment, actually a complete lack of judgment by me. Was it status, materialism, and the opinions of others that brought this on? I shook my head in disbelief. Surely I knew better than that!

The days and weeks drew on with no contact from my attorney and absolutely no luck finding employment. I had been without a job since January 15th, and it was March 16th; over two months, no job prospects, interviews, or callbacks. I had built a spreadsheet of resumes and applications for employment that I had sent out, following up with phone calls at the three-day time frame to insure they received my application, and again two weeks later to let them know I was still very interested in employment. I responded to newspaper ads, online employment Web sites, potential job openings relayed to me by friends, contacted numerous employment agencies, and taken an extensive amount of typing and computer literacy testing, all to no avail.

Employment agencies wanted to know why I left the railroad; when I told them I had been terminated, they were no longer interested. Follow-up phone calls to human resource departments led to the same words, over and over, true or not, " . . . Mr. Grauer, you appear to be over qualified for the position you are applying for" or "Mr. Grauer we can't even come close to meeting the salary requirements of your last employment."

I finally began cold calling human resource departments and setting up informational interviews to find out more about what it takes to become employed, the length of time it may take, and what companies were looking for in potential job candidates. My research was no less discouraging than the results obtained to date. I was told by numerous human resource managers that the climate had changed; finding employment on the average in the Omaha area was taking six months to one year for any type of management position. Corporations were carefully screening potential applicants through multiple interviews, background checks, and reference checks. The interview process alone could potentially last up to three months. The job market was literally flooded with applicants for every position. Larger employers, such as ConAgra, West Communications, and Pay-Pal, were receiving upwards of 10,000 applications and resumes per month.

Friends I worked with at the railroad, even those that had given me permission to use their names as references, began to fade away. I called several of them, only to discover that the legal department of the railroad told them that under no circumstances were they to have any contact with me, and, given the situation, they should not be references for me. The phone calls to play golf, go fishing, to attend the numerous sporting events in the Omaha area, or even go out for a beer, disappeared into thin air.

My days consisted of seeking employment by every available means possible during the first four to six hours of the day. Making some lunch for Sara and me, on those occasions when she elected to come home from work and not run "errands," trying to help with the cleaning, laundry, dishes, grocery shopping, and yard work generally comprised the remainder of the daytime hours. In the evenings, it was the usual hustle and bustle of the kids' activities. On those nights when nothing was scheduled, watching TV alone in the living room was the norm. I had way too much time to contemplate, to worry, and to imagine all of the possible horrific outcomes of my idiocy.

Powerful feelings of emptiness and isolation began to take over. It was more than just wanting company, or wanting to do something with another person. I began to feel cut off, disconnected, and even alienated from my family, friends, people in general, and from God, whom I felt had abandoned me. I began to feel that any type of meaningful human contact was nonexistent. I no longer felt good about myself, when I was alone, because it seemed to me that I was not making good use of my time. As I focused more on what I felt others thought of me, and how I couldn't relate to anyone given all that had transpired, a real fear of total rejection became increasingly prominent. This in turn fed my anxiety levels because I had lost the ability to see how I could be happy without any of the self-defining concepts I previously had held in high regard, such as being popular, well-liked, married, or a leader. As the days went by, both my mental and physical capacities began to diminish; I began to withdraw into my own little world, away from everyone, and I was satisfied to merely wait for the other shoe to drop.

My life with Sara had grown more despondent, dramatically so over the past two months. I needed to hear and feel the sincerity in the words "I love you." Instead, I had to ask, but heard emotionless, routine words. I needed to know that she would stand beside me, support me, and see this through to the end with me. Intimacy, romance, and pretty much any type of physical relationship became nonexistent. Arguments began to intensify; nineteen years of marriage had allowed us to discover one another's "buttons." For both of us, it was becoming easier to say or do something mean, that would hurt the other person. While I knew Sara was deeply hurt and felt a huge sense of betrayal, attempts to discuss her emotions were met with anger, and she seemed to internalize her emotions, going to great lengths to avoid conflict and emotional discussions.

I hadn't realized how unattached we had really become until Sunday, April 15th, the Sunday following our son's eighteenth birthday. This Sunday was no different than many in the past. Everyone was awake by 9:30 a.m. and preparing to go to church. The routine for Sara and I seemed to be set. While one of us was getting dressed and ready to face the day, the other was in the kitchen, drinking a cup of coffee, reading the newspaper, or doing what was necessary to keep the kitchen clean.

The church service began at 10:45 a.m.; we were seated and ready for the service to begin. I bowed my head and prayed that God would open my heart so that I could listen, to make the right decisions, say the right words, and know what direction to take with my life. Just prior to the congregational prayers for church members' needs, prayers of thanksgiving, and the Lord's Prayer, the Pastor had an altar call to share concerns, needs for prayer and healing, and needs for direction and guidance. I am not sure what came over me, but I felt a strong need to share with our church congregation a portion of my past and ask for prayer.

As I stood in front of the congregation and was handed the microphone by our pastor, I began to shake, and for as many times as I had done presentations in front of CEOs, vice-presidents, and senior managers, I became extremely nervous. What was I going to say? What would the reaction be?

"For those of you that don't know me, my name is Dan Grauer, a former employee of the railroad. I am here, in front of you today, to ask for your prayers, guidance, and directions. You see, due to my own stupidity, selfishness, and greed, I threw away a twenty-year career. I was a third-generation railroader." My eyes clouded over and tears began to run down my cheeks. "I have victimized my family and put them in a position I would wish on no one. I am, however, trying to right this wrong, but the mountains that need climbing seem way too high to climb right now; I also know that now is not the time to fail."

Pastor Craig, who at this time had already known the events of the past months, stood beside me with his arm around me for support. I handed him the microphone and began to walk toward my seat, wiping away the tears. He invited me to pray at the altar. I turned and asked Sara to come and join me. I was stunned and heartbroken when Sara looked into my eyes and said, "NO!" I had not realized, nor comprehended, the level of separation our relationship had just reached, but I knew that I was deeply hurt and confused.

With each passing day, I seemed to become less and less interested in seeking employment, only to get the same response. I called the attorney every two weeks for an update and his response was always the same. "Dan, I haven't heard a word from the U.S. Prosecutor and I am not going to push it. The more time that goes by, the better off you're going to be."

By, May 4, I had sent out over 250 resumes and job applications, made 185 follow-up phone calls, and 360 cold calls to various employers in a futile attempt to find employment. I had received a stack of rejection letters and cards that stood at least six inches high off the table top, and another stack that was equally high, stating, "Thank you for applying. Your application is being considered. If you are the most qualified candidate, you will be contacted within the next two to three weeks by our human resources department. Your application will remain on file for ninety days."

My days and nights seemed to be turned around. I would go to bed when the rest of family did in the evenings, but would lay awake for hours. I began taking naps during the day, which in turn led to me sleeping more than ten to twelve hours a day during a twenty-four hour period. My appetite was inconsistent and always at opposite ends of the spectrum. On certain days, I would rarely eat, and during others, there wasn't enough food in the house to satisfy my hunger. I began to lose my concentration and the desire to find employment. The only activity I kept interest in, for the kids, was as commissioner of the girls softball league.

At least twice a week, I found myself in the bathroom, nauseated and sick to my stomach, occasionally with blood in the toilet.

I had hit a new all time low mentally, physically, and spiritually. My comfort came in self-pity, emotional manipulation, and rationalization for how I ended up in this position. Dissatisfaction in my marriage to Sara, brought on by a total breakdown in communication, a lack of trust by Sara, and an absence of physical affection, only fueled the escalating conflict, both internally and in my relationships with others.

Eventually, I began to look for comfort in other avenues; the computer became my best friend. While I continued to search for employment, the chatrooms took the place of friends in looking for someone to listen, the thousands of pages of erotic pictures took the place of intimacy, and the endless computer games took the place of any other type of mental challenge. I was trapped in a mind-set and body I didn't know, but was also blinded by the slow transgression to what was happening; my self-esteem soon followed. I was not a good husband, father, and provider because that was someone who was successful. Men didn't cry and mope around; of course, a real man would not have done what I did. A good husband and father would have maintained control, but not me. I began to convince myself that, "My family would be better off without me, and that just maybe I wouldn't be around when the law finally decides to catch up to me."

Chapter 13

By June 1, my personal descent had become obvious. I had quit sending out resumes and job applications. Sleeping and being at the computer usually comprised twenty of the twenty-four hours in a day. I seldom shaved and had packed on some serious weight. Simply put, I had become an apathetic, self-destructive slob. My roller coaster of emotions was entering dangerous a downswing.

That particular night, after the family had gone to bed, I went back to the computer in the dining room. I was feeling depressed beyond what I thought anyone should have to live through; serious thoughts of suicide crept into my mind and took control. I went back to the bedroom, knelt down, and from underneath the bed took out the deer-hunting rifle that had been given to me by a long-time friend. I walked with it back to the computer, laid it down beside the chair, just staring at it, wondering if I had the guts to do it.

Somewhere over the next hour or so, I convinced myself that this was indeed the way to go, but I needed to tell someone, I needed someone to listen. I took the rifle from its case, loaded it with one round, and laid it back down on the floor. Twice during the next fifteen to twenty minutes, I took the rifle, placed the end of the barrel in my mouth, and fingered the trigger guard. I can't begin to describe the feeling. I lay the rifle down one more time and thought about just how easy this would be.

I logged onto the computer and entered a chatroom, needing to justify to anyone willing to listen my thought processes. As I began typing, I received an intriguing response from someone whose screen name was, "Lonely-not-dumb." That person said they had been in a similar situation, probably worse, and that there was nothing I could ever say that would make suicide an option. Whoever this was hadn't walked at all in my shoes. I was going to convince this person that my world was worse than anyone else's.

It didn't happen! Over the course of the next two hours, I heard about a lady whose husband was in prison for the second time. It was as though I had been cast under some type of spell. I was mesmerized, listening to how she stood by a husband who had broken the law, not once, but twice, leaving her in a marriage now as a single mother to raise their children of ages eleven, thirteen, and seventeen. She and her family had lost all their finances, their home, the car had been repossessed, the kids were devastated and acting out, they were judged and ridiculed by the community, and yet she maintained her faith in God, and had survived.

Just as quickly, as the thoughts of suicide had entered my mind, they dissipated, and my problems didn't seem to be as extreme as they had been earlier in the evening. For the first time in a very long time, I was focused on someone other than me. I don't remember how long we talked in the chatroom, but I know that when I logged off the computer, I looked down at the rifle, slowly picked it up, unloaded it, slid it back into its case, and put it back under the bed. Whoever this person was, I believe they had just saved my life.

I awoke the next morning still thinking about the chatroom discussion from the previous night. I knew the highs and lows would continue, and that at any time new waves of depression might invade my mind, but I also knew that I wanted to win, that if this lady could endure all that she had, I could do it as well. For the first time in a very long time, I was looking forward, not backward, and outside the scope of my own little world.

I had always heard that happiness in life is based 99 percent on the attitude of the person; I didn't believe it. However, life did begin to improve with a change in attitude, if only by baby steps, during the following week. I had my first two real job interviews. The first was with one of the largest trucking companies in America as a claims examiner handling personal injuries; the duties included handling high exposure liability claims for settlement and/or trial in a timely manner. It would include investigating and determining liability, reviewing exposure, analyzing damages for bodily injury claims, negotiating settlements, identifying subrogation potential, and assigning and monitoring insurance adjusters and defense counsel. However, the job also included traveling to and participating in mediations and trials; I wasn't sure I was ready to travel again.

The second employment opportunity was as a Senior Career Advisor for a career placement company within the Omaha area. Job responsibilities included assisting clients with career management, marketing, and developing skills necessary to successfully engineer an employment campaign, entailing evaluation, analysis, and validation of client skills, talents, and experience. Oral and written communication skills were of high priority, including the ability to write and format "eye-catching" client resumes and provide in-depth, detailed training with regard to successful interviewing skills. Given all of the difficulties I had in the recent months, I wasn't sure I was at all well-qualified for ths position.

The job interviews went really well. I was confident that if I could get a face-to-face interview, I would succeed in gaining employment. I did not have a good feeling about the claims examiner position, merely because while I felt that I could fulfill all of the required job responsibilities, I did not have experience in the worker's compensation arena. The laws that were more applicable to my job history with the railroad were federal, and completely different in personal injury interpretation. Additionally, trucking is truly a very different transportation industry than the rail industry.

I was offered the position of Senior Career Advisor based on my communication skills, my past training skills, and the methodologies of "thinking outside the box by establishing informational interviews" I had utilized during my current career search. This position offered a base salary plus commission; benefits were available, but paid solely by the employee. I was excited to simply have a job offer and accepted to start immediately on June 11.

In addition, during the past week, I was able to find "Lonely-not-dumb," in the chatrooms late in the evenings during the week. I was intrigued by her attitude toward life and her reliance on her faith to carry her through. I asked quite literally hundreds of questions and many times heard words of harsh reality in response:

Dan: "I think my wife is so angry with everything that has transpired over the past six months, it is having a huge negative impact on our marriage."

Lonely-not-dumb: "She has every right to be angry. She is a victim based on what little you have told me. I can't begin to describe how

pissed-off I was, and, for that matter, still am at my husband. The bond
of trust has been broken and that is something that is earned, not given."

Dan: "What about the kids? Were they just as angry?"

Lonely-not-dumb: "Yes, they too have the right to be angry. The difference with the kids is that their love is unconditional, and no matter
how hurt, angry, and disappointed they are, they will come around in time
to forgive and accept."

Dan: "So, how do you regain the trust of your partner?"

Lonely-not-dumb: "You can't, unless both of you are willing to forgive and change. Notice, I said forgive, not forget. I have forgiven my
husband but I am still pissed-off, and have not, nor will I ever forget. In
my case, I am not sure I can ever trust again, because I was promised after
the first bump in the road that this type of thing would never happen
again, but it did.

"Through all of the professional   counseling I have gone through, in
addition to a support group through my church, I have learned I need to
control my anger, not let the anger control me. If I can do this, I believe
we can move forward as a couple, but I am not sure that I am ready to do
that   yet."

Dan: "So, saying you're sorry isn't enough. Trying to make right the
wrongs isn't enough. Taking full responsibility and accountability for the
actions that caused the screw-up isn't enough. Knowing all of the pain,
hurt, and anguish I have caused isn't enough. Is that what you're saying?"

Lonely-not-dumb: "Not at all. My husband has not yet, and I don't
know if he will ever take responsibility for his actions. What I am saying,
is that it takes time, both partners, hard work, and a willingness to change
to get through any situation that has had a major negative impact on a
relationship.

"If you and your wife want to get through this, you need to seek professional counseling. You both have to be willing to lay ALL of the issues
on the table and make changes. If BOTH of you are not resolved to
make the relationship work,   regain what has been lost, re-establish
boundaries in your relationship, forgive and build toward a future together. . . it will never work."

Through subsequent chatroom discussions, I learned that "Lonely-not-
dumb" was a social worker with the state of Iowa, had a degree in psychology, and had experienced a similar "stupid-husband" period that
caused a tremendous amount of hurt and disappointment. The discus-

sions were never specific, but I quickly sensed, based on her experiences, she could answer many of my questions regarding what the future might hold, such as: How long might it take for the government to decide to prosecute, and, if they do, would they arrest me in front of my family? How long can it take between the arrest and the trial? If I was found guilty, would I immediately go to prison? How did her family react? What are the prisons like?

I began to depend on "Lonely-not-dumb" to calm my fears, provide possible answers of future expectations, and a reality check that whatever was in store for me, wasn't going to be easy on me, or my family. We began to chat online three to four nights a week.

On June 29, I received my first paycheck. I don't remember how much it was, but I do remember the feeling of being able to contribute to the well-being of my family. Our finances were wearing extremely thin, and Sara and I had discussed taking out a second mortgage on the house, in order to keep paying the bills and catch-up on some that had fallen behind. Sara had taken a second job, which combined with the kids' summer activities, we seldom, if ever, took time for each other. Our discussions were more like questions followed by one-word answers; the arguments, mostly about money, had intensified, and it seemed as though we went to bed mad and woke up mad at one another more often than not. Physical contact was out of the question; it had been six months.

I met with my attorney almost monthly, and contacted him by telephone every couple of weeks. In our last telephone discussion, he said, "Dan, don't worry. The U.S. Prosecutor hasn't forgotten about you. They are busy with a huge number of criminal cases, and, honestly, it wouldn't surprise me if we didn't formally hear anything until fall."

The waiting game of not knowing what the future held regarding possible criminal charges, or prison time, magnified the family stress, as well as the growing separation and discontent in my relationship with Sara.

My online discussions with Joyce, "Lonely-not-dumb," continued; she gave permission for me to send e-mails with questions and concerns that pertained to what was happening in my life, and I took advantage of that. I had become fascinated and quite honestly attracted to a lady whom I didn't know at all, had never even seen, nor ever met in person. Her ability to communicate her thoughts, emotions, and feelings honestly and openly filled a void that had been created between Sara and I, a void that I needed to have filled.

My "friends" had all seemed to disappear into the woodwork. Sara always seemed too busy working, involved with the kids, or too tired to just sit and talk, and those I came in contact with at work were clients and coworkers, not people that I could confide in. Joyce came across as an intelligent, caring, insightful, and honest woman, who took the time to listen. She was always upfront and challenging, not allowing me to feel sorry for myself by not telling me what I wanted to hear, but the reality of what to expect.

I needed to meet her face-to-face and see this woman who had been able to help change my outlook on life, and who in reality saved my life. July 4 fell on a Wednesday and I was going to take Thursday and Friday as vacation days. As a result of our past e-mail discussions, I discovered that Joyce lived in South Sioux City, Nebraska. I asked her to meet me in Onawa, Iowa, approximately thirty-five miles south of Sioux City, on Friday, July 6, so that I could thank her for all she had done. I think at that point she thought I was truly crazy, but she did agree to the meeting.

We agreed to meet at the McDonald's just off the interstate. Joyce told me that she drove a blue, Ford Taurus and would be there around 10:00 a.m. I promised to buy her a chocolate shake as a token of my appreciation. My gut told me this meeting wasn't the right thing to do, but my heart told me differently. I arrived at the McDonald's in Onawa about 9:45 a.m. I had a ton of questions to ask about how to deal with the kids' feelings, Sara, relatives, and friends. I needed to know how they were dealing with the judgment and criticism from others when impacted by the negativity of a major life event. I was extremely nervous about being judged by Joyce, and being labeled by the biases she had developed from her own past life events.

I was looking at the notepad of paper on the table in front of me with all of my scribbling, when out of the corner of my eye I caught a glimpse of a blue, Ford Taurus with the broken, driver's side mirror pull into the parking area. I watched as out of the car a lady, about 5' 4" or 5" tall, approximately my age, not overweight, but not small, stepped out of the vehicle. Her hair was shoulder length, brownish in color, but had obviously been bleached to a lighter shade by the sun. She wore tan, mid-thigh shorts and a white, short-sleeve shirt with brown stripes in a crisscross fashion throughout the design. Her eyes were covered by glasses, both prescription and clip-on sunglasses. She wore brown sandals that matched perfectly with her well, tanned legs. I watched as she looked around and appeared to recognize my truck as I had described it to her. Then she walked slowly, but cautiously, toward the door. I suspected this was not a typical meeting for her as well.

As she entered the door, I stood up and walked toward her.

"Joyce?"

"Yes, are you Dan?"

"Yes, it's very nice to meet you," I said, giving her a quick hug. "Would you like that chocolate shake I promised?"

I saw a smile that, for the first time in a long while, I knew was genuine, sincere, and full of emotion. "Yes, as a matter of fact I do," she said.

I directed Joyce to where I had been sitting and asked her to join me. She sat in the chair opposite me. Without any other words, I turned toward the counter to place an order for two chocolate shakes. While waiting for our shakes, I turned toward the table and noticed Joyce intently focused on the pad of paper. When I walked back to the table with the shakes in hand, she turned the tablet so that it once again faced me.

"Geez, don't you ever run out of questions?"

"I really appreciate your patience and advice."

"Have you ever been up in this area before?"

"No, these are your stompin' grounds, not mine. There is a lake just on the other side of the interstate. Do you want to go for a drive around the lake, maybe sit at a picnic table and talk?"

"That sounds fine. Let's take my truck."

As we drove, without asking, Joyce began to address some of the issues and concerns I had written down.

"You know, this meeting isn't exactly what a man who wants to save his marriage would do!"

"I have come to trust your judgment and advice. Besides, you have your degree in psychology, right? Bill me."

"Very funny. Just what did you tell your wife?"

I remember that I hemmed-hawed around, changing the subject to her kids, telling her something that I was sure resembled the truth, just not all of it.

We drove around the lake talking for a couple of hours. I found a renewed appreciation for the knowledge, intelligence, and inner beauty this lady so proudly displayed. However, there was aura surrounding Joyce that indicated a guarded or troubled past. I wondered if like many doctors I knew, she was better at giving advice than following it. It was, however, important for me to be able to look into Joyce's eyes and see if the caring, the honesty, and openness were indeed genuine.

I had just experienced one of the most relaxing afternoons I'd had in quite some time. The feeling that I didn't need to hide anything, and that I would not be judged on my past, but on the choices I would elect to make in the future, made me feel good about myself. I felt as though a special friendship had been created with this meeting, that Joyce would be someone I could trust with any and all of my heartfelt feelings and emotions.

I turned back into the McDonald's drive and pulled behind Joyce's car to let her out. As I did so, she took me quite by surprise.

"Dan, I had a good afternoon. I think that we can continue to talk online and exchange e-mails about your upcoming issues and concerns. You do have to realize that I can only give you answers based on my experiences; some of what you want to know needs to be discussed with your attorney, but you have a decision to make. . ."

"What's that?"

"Based on what you have told me, you and Sara need to get into counseling. You have to decide what direction to take your life. It doesn't sound as though you have been satisfied or happy for quite some time in your relationship. If you're looking for me to step in and be an excuse, it won't happen. Oh, and by the way," as she glanced at the golf clubs in the back of my truck, "don't you EVER lie to me again." She walked away, got into her car, and didn't look back.

I was blown away! How could she have known? Was I that transparent? I thought about what Joyce had said the entire way home. I loved Sara, but was I still in love with Sara? Was I willing to continue giving? For the past several years I felt as though I my desires and needs were always on the back burner, that work, money, and the kids were the main priority. Was it anyone's fault, or had we both been so busy going our separate ways that neither one of us had noticed? Were we willing to change or had all the give-and-take disappeared? Had our relationship become like a plant? If not nurtured, watered, and fed the plant dies. Was this true of our relationship?

I was scared, because I never knew of a dead plant ever being resurrected. All I really wanted was for Sara to say that she still wanted me and needed me. Was that so difficult?

Chapter 14

My job was going extremely well. I was on target to bring home about $3,000 in the month of July. It wasn't enough, but it was going to help. I truly enjoyed helping people get in front of decision-makers by formatting a resume that was unique and individual to the personality and profession of that individual. I spent hours working on interviewing skills, such as: how to dress and not to dress, how to shake hands, where to sit, correct body language, what questions could be expected, and what type of answers should be given to those anticipated questions. Just as important was continual contact and follow-up, including a thank-you letter just for an interview. Follow-up phone calls were critical to keep any prospective employers informed of an ongoing interest in working for them. Business cards clipped in the upper right-hand corner of the resume made them stand out when the hiring manager was flipping through a stack of resumes sent by potential employees.

Many clients learned quickly and worked hard to obtain the career they wanted. Others were lazy and didn't want to invest or commit to the necessary time needed to find a career; they just wanted us to call them when there were any pending interviews. As a result, a majority of the clientele was satisfied, but a number of them felt that we were not doing enough to find them a job. I quickly learned that some people truly sought a satisfying, and hopefully long lasting career; others merely wanted a job. No amount of encouragement, direction, or motivation was going to affect a small percentage of our clientele. By August 1, my plate was full; I was working with forty-five clients at any one time, which in order to get the work done, I was required to invest more hours. I began working from approximately 7:30 a.m. until 6:30 p.m., or later, each day.

On the home front, I had tried to talk with Sara on numerous occasions, to tell her how I felt about the rut our relationship had gotten into, and what I hoped we could change. However, it seemed the harder I tried to talk, the more Sara would work to avoid any type of conflict. Maybe that was the problem, maybe I was doing all the talking and not enough listening, but I was trying. I had become extremely frustrated at the total absence of intimacy and romance.

Although, I have to admit, that while in public, we both became extremely proficient at putting on the façade that nothing was wrong. At church and ball games, we sat side by side; we attended teacher's conferences together, and rarely missed any of the kids' events. I don't remember if we had discussed marriage counseling at this point, but I believe that both of us knew that if something didn't change soon, there would be no turning back.

I made time to talk with Joyce in a chatroom or via e-mail because never far from my mind were the pending criminal charges and the potential of prison. I continued to voice my frustrations over my relationship with Sara, and Joyce continued to encourage that I not give up. I don't remember the specific day; however, I know that I was at home and it was late into the night. I was sitting at the computer, and Joyce and I had been in a discussion in a chatroom talking about depression and how it could come and go, its individual effects, how it can affect the family, and all those involved in the life of that individual. I was in the process of typing, " I love your response to the question about the kids" and had managed to type, "I love you" when from behind me I heard, "YOU BASTARD. WHY DON'T YOU JUST LEAVE AND GO TO YOUR WHORE GIRLFRIEND? DO YOU THINK I AM STUPID?"

I turned in the computer chair just in time to see Sara, stomping back down the hallway and slam the bedroom door. I shut the computer off and headed for the couch in the basement. I wasn't sure that any amount of explanation could fix what had just occurred.

Needless to say there wasn't a great deal of sleep to be had that night. I got off the couch around 5:30 a.m. and walked upstairs to shower and get ready for work. Sara was awake as well, lying in bed watching the news. The look on her face told me now was not the time to try and discuss anything, but in typical man-style, I was determined to try.

"Sara, what you saw last night was not the entire conversation."

"I don't want to hear it. I have no reason to believe you or trust anything you say."

"Sara, that's not fair. I have tried to talk with you and you seem to continue to ignore me."

"Well, it's going to get worse before it gets better."

"What does that mean?"

"If you want a divorce, you'll get one."

Those words had never entered into any conversation we'd had until that time, and I was caught off guard by hearing them now.

"Don't you think we should try some counseling and see if we can get back on track?"

"How the hell can we afford that? I don't know that it will do any good anyway."

"Sara, I would like to try. Would you at least go if I could get it set up through the church or something?"

No answer. Sara got out of bed, walked to the kitchen for a cup of coffee, and no further discussion was held that morning, about anything.

At work, I called our church and learned that there were counseling services offered by a community counseling group funded primarily by grants, churches, and private donation. I called and set up our first appointment for the following Monday evening at 4:30 p.m. with a counselor by the name of Madison. I gave Madison a brief history of what had taken place over the past two years, leaving nothing out. She asked a few questions, and asked what my expectations of the counseling were. I responded that I wasn't sure, but that if Sara and I could find a way to get back on the same page and share the same dreams for our future, I would like to try and save our twenty-year marriage. She asked if I was willing to make changes in order to get that accomplished. I agreed without any hesitation.

I e-mailed Joyce to tell her all that had taken place. She apologized profusely for what happened, stating over and over again that she did not want to be the reason behind the end of a marriage. I told her it was not her fault, that the timing of everything just really sucked, and it was my hope that counseling could guide Sara and I back on track.

I told Sara about our appointment at the church. I don't remember her response, but I remember the skepticism and doubt, although she actually agreed to take off work a little bit early to make the appointment. In our initial discussions, Madison had said this was not going to be an easy fix, that it would take commitment, work, and change by both Sara and I. I was willing to give it a try, but I didn't know about Sara.

On Monday afternoon, I left work about 4:00 p.m. for our appointment with Madison. As I drove to the church, I kept thinking about the changes I would be willing to make, what I would give up, and what I felt was truly important in maintaining our relationship. Sara had not yet arrived when I pulled into the parking lot. I stepped out of the car and entered the back door of the church where Madison had told me her office was located. I looked around as I stepped in the door and realized, that as many years as we had attended this church, I did not know this area was located there. Madison's door was open and I stepped into the doorway. Madison was a woman in her late twenties to mid-thirties. She had long, dark hair in a ponytail, hanging to the middle of her back. She reminded me of a long-haired Rosanne Barr.

"Hi, are you Dan?"

"Yes, Ma'am."

"Is Sara here with you?"

"No, not yet, but she is on her way, I'm sure."

"Well, here is some preliminary paperwork I need you to complete as thoroughly as possible." As she continued she handed me a clipboard with several documents. "I spent a bit of time talking with you on the phone and would like to spend a majority of this appointment talking with Sara, so that we can develop a game plan on how to proceed."

"O.K., I have no problem with that. I can complete the paperwork while you and Sara are meeting, once she gets here."

About that time, Sara walked through the door and I introduced her to Madison. Madison and Sara shook hands and Madison essentially repeated what she had told me. Sara and Madison disappeared behind a closed office door, leaving me standing in the small reception area. I sat down and began on the all-inclusive paperwork history.

Just as I was completing the last required document, the door opened, and Madison stepped out. I glanced at my watch, and it had been about forty minutes since Sara had entered the office.

"Dan, I would like you to join us."

"O.K.," I said. I stood, handing the clipboard to Madison as I walked through the door. Sara was seated on a couch on the far side of the office; I sat in a chair that was on the wall perpendicular to Sara, but still faced

Madison's desk. Nothing was said for a few minutes, as Madison appeared to be reviewing her notes. She then looked up and looked me squarely in the eyes.

"Dan, based on what both you and Sara have told me, you are going to need to deal with several issues. Sara is going to be angry. She does not currently trust you and that is a real issue. Sara has been deeply hurt. Secondly, I understand that you are having an affair with a lady from Sioux City; you didn't tell me that. You know I just came out of a relationship under almost the same circumstances, so I can understand what Sara is feeling. My personal life is not relevant other than I know the amount of work this is going to take. Immediate decisions and changes will need to be made if you want to save your marriage."

Oh my God! I couldn't believe my ears. This was not an independent counseling session, but an ambush based on feelings!

"O.K. First off, just how do you define affair?"

"Well, in the literal sense it can be any contact with a person of the opposite sex where there is a sharing of emotion that would normally have been shared with a spouse."

"If that is your definition of affair, then yes, I am guilty."

"What is this lady's name?"

"Joyce Treadway."

"Dan, before we can proceed any further you need to stop all contact with Joyce, period."

"Now wait a minute. I have NO ONE else to talk with, share my frustrations, emotions, and needs. Sara is too busy working and doing other things to take the time to listen. I have tried to talk with her about the same issues discussed with Joyce. I currently have no friends on which to rely. I have embarrassed my family and relatives. What I have pending is continually hanging over my shoulder. Joyce has been through a similar situation and can share accurate expectations of what to expect. She has done nothing but support Sara. Just whom should I turn to?"

"You need to rely on Sara. She tells me she is working so much in order to support the family."

"I agree, but has Sara told you that she has been to only one of six attorney appointments because she refuses to take off work, or that since January of this year, there has been virtually no intimacy, romance, or love, or that just in order to hear the words 'I love you,', I have to ask?"

"This isn't about Sara. She is a victim here. You need to make some serious adjustments if you want to save this marriage, and that is what you want, isn't it?"

"Yes, it is, but I thought this was about both of us changing. I need to know what changes Sara is willing to make, what is she willing to give up in order to save the marriage."

"Dan, you need to be the one to start the ball rolling, and if you don't want to, then you need to make that decision and we can continue counseling for both of you in preparing for divorce."

Holy shit! What had I gotten myself into? I am trapped and I am going to be the bad guy no matter what decision I make.

"Well, I am not going to make any decision today. I need to think about what I have just heard. I believe with all my heart that changes need to be made by both Sara and I, not just me. I need to hear a commitment from Sara. Is she willing to change as well?"

"Based on what she has told me, I believe the answer is yes."

"Then why can't she tell me? Why can't she tell me that she will be there to support me, to love me, and nurture this relationship? Why can't she show me some tenderness and compassion?"

"Because she is extremely angry right now."

"Madison, we can talk about this all day long, but I will not make a decision today without hearing what changes Sara is willing to make as well."

"Well, I believe you are compromising your relationship then. Let's take some time and make another appointment for next week."

"O.K." I agreed, just relieved to get out of this meeting.

I walked out of the church, went directly to my truck, and left. I was livid the entire way home. I had vowed to limit my contact with Joyce to chatrooms and e-mail, but I picked up my cell phone and called her. I told her all that I heard and how I interpreted the meeting. Her only response was, "Sara is really angry and does have every right to be. I do think your counselor is beyond objective and has a bias favoring Sara."

"Gee, do ya think so? What do I do?"

"I can't make that decision for you. I will abide by whatever decisions you make. I am not going to contact you unless you initiate the contact. Once again, I am NOT going to be the reason for ending a marriage."

Later in the evening, as I sat in the living room watching TV, and Sara was on the love seat reading the newspaper, I tried to talk about the afternoon therapy session.

"Are you comfortable with Madison as our therapist?"

Sara lowered the newspaper and looked over the top it. "I suppose you're not because she sided with my point of view; what do you want to do, keep changing therapists until you find one that sides with you?"

"I didn't say that. I asked if you were comfortable with Madison as a therapist. Do you think she can adequately or successfully conduct the counseling we need to make this work?"

"Well, it doesn't sound like you want to give up Joyce, so I don't expect you to change."

"Will you please just answer my question?"

The newspaper went back up and not another word was said. I stood up and went to the computer.

"I suppose you're going to get online and tell your little whore everything."

"Yep, you got it! That's exactly what I am going to do."

In order to avoid the confrontations at home, I began to work more and more hours. I would sometimes go to work as early as 7:00 a.m. and work until 8:30 p.m. or later. I knew that this wasn't fair to the kids, but neither was it fair that they see Sara and I argue all of the time. I continued to sleep on the couch in the basement. The kids seemed caught in the middle, though Sara and I both continued to tell them how much we loved them.

We continued going to therapy either every week or every two weeks. I continued to feel as though I was the one that was doing everything wrong in our marriage. We both wrote letters to one another, but shared them only with Madison, in an attempt to document our discontent and frustration. The focus always seemed to be that I quit talking with Joyce before anything else would happen. I always retorted with a need for commitment on the part of both Sara and I. I felt that no real progress was being made, but if Sara could vent and voice her anger, maybe she could begin to heal, at least that was my hope.

September snuck up on us quickly and our son, Ryan, was preparing to go off to college at the University of Chicago. I was both excited for him and sad at the same time. Ryan had earned his way into one the most prestigious universities in the United States and academically qualified for numerous financial awards. Both Sara and I were extremely proud of him.

I will never forget how the University arranged for the parents to say "goodbye" and let go of their sons and daughters. Following a morning of speeches, introductions, and tours of the University, lunch was provided. After lunch, the students and parents walked hand in hand down one of the main streets of the University behind the blaring bagpipes of the University color guard. As we approached the end of the street, there was a "Y" in the road; students were directed to the left toward the dorms and parents were directed to the right toward the parking lots. As we shared our final hugs, kisses, and tears, I couldn't help but wonder if the next time Ryan saw his parents if we would still be "together."

I did have to give credit to Sara, in that we both worked hard in trying not to argue and fight in front of the girls. I am not sure that we were able to totally hide our feelings for one another, but we had resorted to being tolerable of one another when around the girls.

Counseling continued, and finally at the end of September, Madison said, "We are not making progress here. You need to make a decision on whether you want to continue working toward saving your relationship, or focus our counseling on an amicable separation. Dan, what do you want to do?"

"Wait a minute. Why is this MY decision? Shouldn't it be OUR decision?"

"You appear to be the one who is walking the fence line and you need to move one way or the other."

"And what type of commitment has Sara made?"

"We can have this discussion all day, but by our next appointment, October 10, we need to decide."

The week was an extremely long one. It seemed as though every time Sara and I tried to have a discussion about our relationship, it turned into a knockdown-drag-out that always involved Joyce and the fact that I put the family in this situation. I began to believe that Sara harbored so much anger there was going to be no forgiveness, no trust, and certainly no change toward anything that I suggested would make the relationship better. I guess I couldn't blame her; I had really messed things up this time.

The drama peaked during the next week when the counseling session began with Madison saying, "Dan, I feel as though you haven't been truthful with me, and I don't feel that you want to save the relationship with Sara. As such, I can no longer be a therapist for you. I have called Rachel Banning, another counselor at St. Andrew's United Methodist Church on Maple Street; she has agreed to take over your personal therapy needs. I will continue to work with Sara and the kids as they feel I am needed."

I was speechless and I guess there was nothing else to say. I got up, left, and moved out of the house the next week, moving into a basement apartment in a house located in LaVista, Nebraska, approximately a mile away from our home.

Sara kept saying, "Once you move out, we're done," and, "So, I suppose that bitch from Sioux City is going to move in with you." I couldn't take anymore ridicule and anger.

Taking only the bare essentials and some of the furniture from the basement, I left Sara with all the new furniture, appliances, household furnishings, tools, and anything else that had been purchased with "kickback" monies. In my heart all I ever really wanted was to have Sara say that she was willing to fight for our marriage, that we could work together to resolve our differences, that she loved me, would stand by me, and that she was willing to change; however, I was tired of being both the monster and the beating post for all that had gone wrong in our marriage during the course of the last five years.

Chapter 15

My apartment was really small. The entryway led immediately into the living room area. The bedroom was big enough for a full-size bed, one dresser, and just enough room to get out of bed and take one step before reaching the closet. A bathroom, with a small shower that was barely big enough to turn around in, was just off the living room area. An extremely small kitchen that included a washer and dryer filled the remaining basement area. The walls and ceilings were painted white, nothing fancy but livable.

I sat on the couch facing an old television, staring at it as though entranced by whatever was on, but my mind was elsewhere. It was October 19; two days past what would have been our twenty-year anniversary. I buried my face in a pillow and cried! I felt as though I had really tried. I worked hard to give Sara and the kids everything they wanted and more, and yet it had never seemed enough. I was a failure as a husband and a father. Sara was right!

During the last two months, my emotions had felt like a yo-yo, one minute being extended as far as possible and pushing the outer limits of the string and the next wound tight and straining to wind even more string around the central core. I had taken an old computer from our storage shed and had hooked up the Internet; although it was extremely slow, it sufficed for my needs. I continued to talk via chatrooms and e-mail with Joyce and had begun talking with her almost daily on the telephone. I think that had Joyce billed me for all of the hours she fulfilled in the role as my psychologist, she most certainly would have been able to buy a new car. She seemed to accept me for who I was, both good and bad. Joyce obviously disagreed with my decision-making of the past few years, but at the same time, she made me feel as though I had a future. A very special bond had developed between us, one that I had not experienced for quite some time, based on openness and acceptance. I truly appreciated the honesty and sincerity of her words and emotions.

Joyce felt obligated to tell me how she felt having been victimized by her husband, not once but twice. She needed to know the thought process behind "why" I made the decisions I had in my own crime so that she could in some logical sense try and apply it to her own relationship. It was almost as if she would attempt to rationalize her husband's thought processes for what he had done to their family.

Joyce drove from South Sioux City to LaVista the evening of November 10. We planned on having dinner and doing what we had for the past several months: talking about our common experiences, what we could change, what we could not, and where we would like our future to go. With the possibility of prison hanging over my head, and Joyce's husband already having been in prison for quite some time, I don't believe that either one of us wanted to look too far into the future. The one discussion that seemed almost consistent in content was our current partners; we had both come to the realization that people don't change unless they want to, no matter how hard we might want them to. Neither of us were yet willing to admit to giving up, but we were in the same boat, rowing in the same circle.

I had just looked at my watch; it was about 6:00 p.m. when I heard a soft knock on my door.

"The door's unlocked. Come on in."

"Hi, kid! How ya doing?" I turned just in time to see a bright, sunshine-like smile on a face that simply glowed with happiness. Joyce walked through the door with a sack of groceries in each arm. She looked around the tiny apartment as she continued to walk through to the small kitchen as though she owned the place.

"It's been a long week. I need to have a good weekend. How about you?"

"Honey, it has been a long week, and I am going to cook you a dinner you'll never forget." I remember the first time Joyce called me "honey." I thought I was really special until I realized that everyone involved in her life was a honey also, even people she had never met before.

"What's for supper?"

"Well, you've been whining about wanting chicken and dumplings so that's what we're going to have."

"Cool. What can I do to help?"

For the next hour we stood side by side in my small, quaint kitchen, cutting up celery, onions, chicken, and putting together homemade egg noodles. We discussed how our week went at work, our kids, and the emotional roller coaster I had been feeling with my family. When the stockpot was put on the stove to boil, we went into the living room and sat on the couch watching television. Nothing was said for a few minutes, but then our lives changed dramatically.

I turned toward Joyce, took her hand in mine, and looked deep into her eyes. With tears running down my cheeks, I tried to thank her for all she had done, to tell her that she had quite literally saved my life. She put a finger to my lips. . .

"Shhh. ."

"Joyce, I. . .uh. . ."

"Dan, there's no need to say anything, I already know."

I scooted closer to her side and hugged her as though it would be the last hug I gave to anyone. I held on for what seemed a very long time, surprised that her response was equally intense. We slowly separated, and as our lips passed close to one another's, a deep, passionate kiss began. The softness of her lips and lightening in her eyes was something I had not felt or seen in almost a year. Both of us were overcome with a renewed feeling of excitement and intensity that I thought was all but forgotten. The desire for a physical release and the spontaneity turned our magnetism and affection into an uncontrolled, unplanned, but unforgettable love-making session.

Later that evening following dinner, we tried to talk about what had taken place, and what it meant to each of us. It was obvious that our feelings resembled a ball of yarn: guilt, pleasure, affection, need, fear, and anxiety were a few of the emotions intertwined.

"Joyce, it's been a very long time since a woman made me feel like a man, like I was wanted and needed; I can't begin to describe what I am feeling. Thank you."

"Well, I kinda enjoyed it myself, you know."

"I know that our relationship has began to take on new meaning for me."

"What do you mean? I am not planning on leaving my husband, and I don't believe for a minute that you have totally given up on your relationship with Sara."

"I know that, but you need to know that the openness and willingness with which we talk and share our feelings is something I am not used to, and I don't know what to do about it."

"Well, have you tried to talk with Sara about it?"

"I have, lots of times. We would talk about how I felt our relationship was in a rut; that I felt we had so many irons in the fire my feelings were always getting put on the back burner; that we didn't take time for "us" anymore."

"And what does she say?"

"Really not much of anything. Sara listens and things get better for awhile but she doesn't tell me anything. I can't read her mind, and when I ask her to share her feelings and emotions, she becomes frustrated with me."

"Dan, you are going to have to decide what you want your future to look like. If you want to get back with Sara, then you have to be willing to accept the fact that she may never change. You have to be willing to continue to give, and if receiving isn't reciprocated, then live with it. If that's not what you want then, you have to decide what your future is going to look like. What I do know is this: I am not going to stand between you and Sara, or you and your family!"

"So, what just took place was a physical release and nothing more?"

"I can't say that. I felt the same passion and desires you did. I am not proud of what we did, but damn it, I enjoyed it. What I am saying is, our fate is in God's hands and on God's time line, not ours. Don't try to control something you can't. What you can do is make choices and stick by them, but they have to be choices you make."

"Where do we go from here?"

"One day at a time, Dan. That's the only way I have survived the past few years, and looking forward too far scares the hell out of me."

Saturday afternoon, as I watched Joyce drive away, I had discovered a new appreciation for living one day at a time and living that day to its fullest, and a much deeper respect for Joyce's knowledge, perspective on life, and faith in God.

Sara and I took the kids to my parents' house for Thanksgiving. The trip from Omaha, to Marysville, Kansas takes about two hours and fifteen minutes. You could count on one hand the number of words exchanged between Sara and I during the drive. The radio was shut off and Sara was reading the newspaper. The kids were preoccupied reading or listening to music; each had their own portable CD player and headset. Occasionally, when they listened to the music loud enough, three separate distinct types of muffled music could be heard, as though it were a competition to drown out the music from another part of the vehicle.

"So, do you want to talk?"

Silence. I decided I was going to talk anyway, she could damn well listen.

"Sara, I love you. We have been married for twenty years that by itself should count for something. We have struggled for the past five years, and it's time for something to change if our relationship is going to survive. I admit that my decision-making over the past few years has been deplorable, but every bit of money has been spent on trying to make things better for you and the kids."

Silence.

"Sara, what do you want me to say? I have tried to talk about our relationship and how I feel we have grown apart; I have tried to talk about us, and the need for dedicated time to one another; I am still in love with you, but I can't do this anymore. I need you to support me, stand by me, and show me that you still love me. Do you?"

Sara turned away, looking out the passenger side window.

"Sara, damn it, I could possibly go to prison. I am doing the best I can in dealing with this. I don't want to lose my family. Am I that much of a monster?"

Silence. I gave up. The remainder of the drive was filled by country music portraying the journeys of love and lost relationships. I felt like I was a part of that world.

As we pulled into the driveway and slowed to a stop, I did my best Ricardo Montalban imitation from *Fantasy Island:*

"Smiles, everyone! Smiles let the façade begin." I turned to see a couple of daggers being thrown at me by Sara as she got out of the truck and slammed the door.

The weekend was relatively uneventful. Sara seemed to go out of her way to help mom with the cooking and dishes. We slept in the same bed, but no talking, cuddling, or touching was allowed. Eating, naps, football, and Pinochle were the main attractions of the weekend. As usual, mom cooked enough to feed an army, though when our family was together, there were nineteen of us around the table. My brothers and their families knew that Sara and I had separated, but that we were attending marriage counseling. I purposely had not told them everything. I wasn't sure what to say or how to say it. Sunday afternoon arrived all too soon and it was time to head back to home. I cringed at the thought; I had no home, not right now anyway.

The drive back to Omaha was almost a carbon copy of the drive down to my parents; the kids were off in their own little world, although I always wondered if it was by choice or merely an attempt to avoid any discussion of family issues. About halfway home, I looked at Sara. She was starring out the passenger side window, crying.

"What's the matter?"

"My family isn't as close as yours and I am going to miss all of this."

"What are you talking about? It sounds like your mind is made up."

"Well, you don't seem to want to give up Joyce."

"Are you willing to change? It takes both of us to make this work; one person changing doesn't do any good. All I need to hear is that you love me, you will stand by me, and that you will try to change so that our relationship improves. In turn, I will commit wholeheartedly to you and only you, Sara. . ."

Silence. There was no further conversation.

I pulled into the driveway of our home to drop off Sara and the kids before going to the apartment. The kids had headed into the house, and as Sara got out, I grabbed her arm and she looked at me.

"I love you, Sara."

Pulling her arm away with no answer, she turned and walked into the house without a word. I was beginning to believe that I was fighting a losing battle.

With Christmas approaching, I really began to struggle. The holiday blues had set in; work was slow, the kids were busy with all of their activities and didn't have time to visit. Joyce and I talked occasionally, but not as often as we had in the past. Christmas had always been a special time for me; I loved playing Santa Claus. I would go to the schools and hospitals and do numerous private visits, but not this year. I just couldn't bring myself into the true spirit of Christmas. I did go shopping for the kids and for Sara, and, just like all the other years, spent more than I should have, but I really enjoyed giving. As I began to wrap all the gifts, I looked around my little apartment and realized there were absolutely no signs of Christmas: no decorations, no lights, no tree, it just wasn't the same, I missed my family horribly. I began to rethink all that I had said and done over the past months regarding my marriage, my family, and my future. Maybe I was wrong. I screwed up; I had caused all the heartache and pain. Maybe Sara was right, I should be the one to change. Were my expectations of a good marriage too high? All I wanted was "normal," but what is "normal?"

During the last two months, I had been attending counseling every two weeks at St. Mark's United Methodist Church with Rachel Banning. Hours of discussions to include an in-depth look into my past, my current relationships, my marriage, our family, and my thought processes proved exhausting. We had conducted a series of written tests, documentation exercises, and readings geared to identify my emotional status, my decision-making thought process, and my general understanding capabilities. The results weren't surprising to me, but Rachel was able to help me understand why certain traits could result in dramatic and negative impacts in my decision-making.

"Dan, here is a copy of all your testing to date. Read through everything and then we can discuss how all of this applies to you."

"O.K. . ."

I slowly and intently read the results, hoping to identify the "why" in my total loss of integrity over the past few years.

"You tend to take it upon yourself to arrange for the health and welfare of those in your care. You are extremely sociable, and thus are a great nurturer of established institutions, such as schools, businesses, churches, social clubs, and civic groups. You enjoy serving in the role of social contributor, happily giving of your time and energy to make sure that the needs of others are met. You tend to be highly cooperative almost to the point of detrimental. You are outstanding at maintaining teamwork among helpers and will give tireless attention to the details of furnishings, goods, and services. You are able to approach others with ease and confidence and are seemingly aware of what everyone's been doing. You are able to remember people's names, usually after one introduction, and always seemed to be concerned about the needs of others. You enjoy and joyfully observe traditions and are a very liberal giver. While willing to provide service, you expect the same from others.

"You are extremely sensitive to the feelings of others, which leaves you open to being extremely self-conscious and sometimes overly sensitive to what others think about you. You can be easily wounded and crushed by personal criticism, by nature 'wearing your heart on your sleeve,' but when wounded your emotions will not be contained. You are quick to like and dislike, and don't mind saying so. At the same time situations that arise which call for a suspension of criticism will lead you to a loosening of the more rigid rights and wrongs; teasing and slapstick humor often results.

"Your sense of right and wrong will battle and wrestle with an over-whelming rescuing or 'motherly' drive. This can result in swift, immediate action that bypasses all internal warnings of red flags. When a decision must be made, especially one involving extreme risk and conflict, an internal wrestling match between black-and-white, values, and morals ensues. You tend to show extreme amounts of personal loyalty to family, friends, and in the workplace. This loyalty if taken to an extreme can cause conflict."

"So, what I am I supposed to get out of this report?"

"Well, several of the traits that you exhibit can be both good and bad. Your decision-making can be flawed if you can justify a sympathetic reason for overriding values. This will tend to lead into emotional decision-making instead of using logical reason as a basis for your decisions. Additionally, right or wrong, you can be loyal to a fault. We will spend the next several weeks discussing how you can recognize these situations and implement a more cautious approach to your thought processes."

"I guess I still don't understand when an educated person knows right from wrong and is surrounded with a good sense of morality and values, how in the world can the decision-making be so horrible?"

"It happens more often than you think when feelings and emotion control the decision-making process. As I said, we are going to spend the next few weeks discussing the application of this within the context of your life."

I usually felt somewhat better coming out of the counseling sessions than when I went into them, but this one really gave me something to chew on. Before leaving, I made appointments for the next two months giving Rachel enough time to explain and interpret all of the testing.

Chapter 16

It was Christmas Eve and I sat in my apartment alone. Sara and the kids would attend the Christmas Eve church service. This had been a tradition for as long as we had been married. I had planned over and over again in my mind how I hoped Christmas Day would go. I had hoped that Christmas would melt Sara's heart and squelch the fire of anger that brewed. Although the kids were older, they would be up earlier than usual and want to open Christmas presents.

Ryan had come home from college a week or so earlier and he and I had strung the Christmas lights around the house. I knew the importance of Christmas to the kids. We put out all of the Christmas decorations: the dwarfed light-up Santa Claus, snowman, Christmas penguins, candy canes, and unending lengths of garland. After dark, when we plugged the lights in, the house looked as good as it had at anytime in the past.

I had taken all the gifts I had purchased over to the house and placed them under the Christmas tree. The almost mandatory two-liter bottles of Pepsi with a $5 bill rubber banded around them were in place; this was an expected gift covering a span of at least the last ten years. Sara was insistent that she cook her traditional Christmas morning breakfast that included almost every imaginable breakfast food combination. We had agreed that I would come over early Christmas morning; we would unwrap the gifts and eat a late breakfast. I had a feeling that this Christmas was going to be a make it or break it holiday for our marriage.

Although I didn't set an alarm, my eyes popped open at 6:00 a.m. It had become habit to get up, shower, and get ready for the day. Even on days when I could sleep in, the habit was hard to break because my bladder also seemed to have some kind of internal alarm. I got out of bed, showered, and sat on the couch with a hot cup of coffee. I thought about the meaning of Christmas. I hadn't attended church for quite some time, nor had I read the Bible or prayed for that matter. It just didn't seem to matter. I had made a deal with God to tell the truth, all of it, but I didn't expect the consequences to be anything like this. I looked at my watch; it was only 7:00 a.m. so I flipped channels until I found a rerun of *Law and Order* and settled back on the couch for an hour.

I arrived at the house and walked up the outside stairs to the front door. I began to open the door and walk in when I realized that I was no longer a part of this household. A shiver ran down my spine, as for the first time I reached for the door handle and it was locked. I took a slow step back, closed the glass door, and rang the doorbell.

Sara answered the door, wrapped in a baby-blue robe that had seen more than its share of years. The door opened and before I could even say, "Merry Christmas," she turned and walked away. I walked into the living room and sat on the loveseat. I was afraid to ask for a cup of coffee.

The kids came pounding down the hallway with enough noise that a stranger may have expected a herd of horses. Holding onto the wall to turn the corner, Alisha was the first to run to me, grab my neck, kiss me, and say, "Merry Christmas." Tiffany wasn't very far behind with the same warm greeting. I glanced toward the stairway to the basement just in time to see Ryan trudging up the stairs rubbing his eyes, grumbling about how early it was. He did manage a mumbled, "Hey Dad, Merry Christmas." Sara was the last to arrive carrying a cup of coffee. She on the opposite side of the living room with a smile that I wasn't sure was genuine, but was necessary for the kids if nothing else.

We did keep with Grauer family tradition, in that, the youngest passes out all of the Christmas presents and Christmas stockings. After all the gifts had been passed out, we would start with the youngest in opening the Christmas stockings first, then the gifts, and proceed up the age ladder in order. Alisha didn't hesitate to start ripping apart the Christmas wrap, spending only a few minutes with each gift to make sure what it was and pass on a quick "Thanks" to the giver. It seemed that for all of the build-up in anticipation and excitement surrounding Christmas, it took far less time to open the gifts and for Christmas to end.

Tiffany took a little more time opening her gifts and savoring the newness. She passed out "Thank yous," hugs, and kisses once she had opened her last present. Alisha paid no attention to anyone else and was focused on playing with her new "toys."

For whatever reason, the older our children got, the fewer the number of gifts, but the more expensive the gift became. Ryan patiently and methodically opened each gift, slowly tearing the Christmas wrap at each place a piece of tape had been placed. He typically received books, CDs and one special gift, something he had mentioned throughout the year that he really wanted. Ryan was always very appreciative of his gifts, and like Tiffany, passed out hugs and kisses along with a "Thank you."

Like Ryan, Sara would take her time opening each present. She would hold the present high in the air, admire it, then give a hug and kiss to the giver. I had made sure the kids had plenty of money to buy their mom a present or two. I had bought several gifts, including a complete set of Teflon pots and pans that had caught her eye during a shopping trip early in the year. I had hoped the gifts would be the key to opening the doors for a new beginning in our relationship. Sara seemed very pleased with all she received, even managing to tell me "Thanks" for the gifts received from me.

Finally, it was my turn. I took my time making sure each of my children knew how much I truly appreciated the gift. When appropriate, I would tell them exactly where it would set in my office, exactly what I was going to do with it, or when I was going to wear it. I passed out hugs and kisses upon opening each gift as well. When I had opened the last gift set in front of me, I looked at Sara. She was staring at the floor refusing to look at me; she had not given me a Christmas gift. Knowing how much Christmas meant to me, I also knew, as did she, that this would be a major blow to my already dwindling feelings about myself. I shouldn't have been, but I was hurt.......this one cut deep.

I left the house late in the morning. The kids were heading back to bed, as some of the joy and excitement had already worn down. Sara was loading the last of the dishes in to the dishwasher. I gave each of the kids another big hug and kiss, gathered up my gifts, and looked toward Sara.

"Thank you for having me over and for the breakfast."

"Yup." Sara walked down the hallway and to the bedroom.

The remainder of Christmas Day was long. My family was going to get together during the upcoming weekend, Sara's family on the following weekend. My family insisted that Sara and the kids come to Christmas as well. Christmas Day obviously did not turn out as I had hoped, and based on this, I had no expectations for the other two Christmas days still coming. I wasn't sure that I was welcome at Sara's family Christmas, but I was asked to go. I took a couple of Tylenol PM, turned the TV on, and promptly turned into a couch potato.

I don't even know what time it was when I heard a knock at my door. I opened my eyes and tried to shake the sleep out of my head. A quick glance out the basement window revealed it was daylight.

"BANG, BANG, BANG." It sounded like someone was trying to knock the door down.

"Just a damn minute! I'll be there in a second." Whoever was at the door was going to get an earful of my thoughts.

I opened the door and my heart went to my throat. Once again, I saw the ear-to-ear grin, the sincerity, and caring of someone that had began to become special to me in so many ways.

"Merry Christmas, kid! You gonna just let the wind blow up your underwear or are you going to invite me in?"

"Joyce . . .what are you. . .?"

Joyce burst in the door, bulldozing her way by me. She carried a big box right through to the couch and sat it down on the floor. With her hands on her hips, she did a quick assessment of the apartment.

"Not much for Christmas spirit here kid, but we're going to fix that."

Joyce sat on the couch and opened the box. Reaching inside, she stood up and had a small Christmas tree already decorated with lights, tinsel, and miniature glass decorations. She walked over to the TV, sat the tree on top of the television, then reached down and plugged the Christmas tree in. The lights glowed brightly in my dark little basement apartment. The soft glow reflecting off the glass ornaments cast soft shadows onto the ceiling. An angel stood proudly on the top of the tree with her wings spread wide in celebration of the birth of a King.

I hadn't moved from the entryway; it was almost as if my feet were frozen in concrete. I turned and watched Joyce smile with satisfaction and admiration at the small Christmas tree. Overwhelmed with emotion, I just sat down and cried.

"I thought I would cheer you up, not make you cry," Joyce said, as she walked to me, hugged me, and just held me tight as I wept. I didn't know what to say or do. It had seemed so long since someone wanted to give something to me without an expectation in return.

As Joyce's hug began to fade, I looked up, and she was holding a piece of mistletoe over my head. I looked back into her eyes; they were so shiny I could see myself. Without hesitation, Joyce kissed me and gave me another hearty "Merry Christmas."

"You go shower and get ready for a good day. When you get out of the shower I have surprise for you."

I stepped out of the shower and looked into the mirror. I couldn't believe she was here. How could she have known? I opened the door of the bathroom and stepped out into the living room area only to be amazed by what I saw. Joyce had strung lights and put up Christmas decorations throughout the basement apartment. In just a few minutes I was taken from a dark, friendless, solitary world into a warm, caring, and understanding atmosphere by a woman who had no idea that her unconditional giving was making a permanent impact on both of our lives.

"Well, are you going to stand there all day wrapped in a towel? Go, get dressed and come on over and sit down. There's more!"

I could actually feel the smile on my face and it felt good. I walked to the bedroom and quickly dressed with a renewed, kid-like excitement. The minute I sat down next to Joyce, she quickly placed two presents in my lap.

"What's this? Joyce, I didn't . . ."

"Hush. Christmas is about giving, remember?"

"I know, but. . ."

"Dan, just shut up and enjoy the moment."

I picked up the smaller of the two gifts. It was wrapped in white tissue paper with a purple ribbon, Joyce's favorite color. I slowly unwrapped the gift not knowing at all what to expect. Finally, I got down to the core of the wrapping and found a forest, green rock about the size of a quarter, and etched into the rock was the word "Faith." I looked at Joyce with what must have been a look of confusion.

"Dan, Christmas is about God giving us his Son. His Son died for all of our sins, even yours, but you have to have faith that God doesn't make mistakes in anything he does, or faith is useless."

Without saying anything, I picked up the other gift. This present was wrapped in bright red and green Christmas paper. It was a bottle of something; of what, I was about to find out. I began to unroll the wrapping from around the bottle, and before I realized it, I heard myself laughing out loud.

In one of our very first e-mail discussions, Joyce and I talked about brand names and food. I had told her there were three things I insisted on: Hershey's chocolate syrup, Heinz ketchup, and Log Cabin syrup. I was looking at a small bottle of Log Cabin syrup.

"Last time I was here, you didn't have any syrup to make waffles or pancakes. I remembered what you told me. Now, I am going to make you breakfast," and she did.

I sat on the couch staring toward the kitchen. I couldn't help but wonder if what was happening was truly meant to be, or would the other shoe drop at any moment?

During the next two days I felt as though I slept more than I had during the entire month. Joyce was content to read, watch television, and play computer games. We had numerous discussions regarding the feelings of our kids, what the future might hold, both good and bad for both of our families, and the role of God in our lives. Oddly enough, sex wasn't an issue or an occurrence during the two days. Complete contentment for both of us was found through communication and mere touch, intent listening, open discussion pertaining to any issue, and the safe feeling of a physical presence provided the needed fulfillment. When Saturday arrived, I wasn't ready for Joyce to leave, but leave she did and I was thankful to have had quality time where the caring, compassion, affection, and attentiveness was genuine and unrehearsed.

Christmas with my family and with Sara's family appeared normal to everyone, except Sara and I. We had become quite good at displaying a pretence of contentment within our relationship to all those who were a part of our lives. I don't think either one of us wanted to admit that we had become like two bulls fighting for dominance, butting heads, and pawing at the ground, hoping that the other would collapse and give in. Both of us felt betrayed by the other's unwillingness to change, the lack of communication, and the fear of what the future might hold.

Sara had lost her trust in me. She was outraged with the thought that we might lose everything, our current life style and possibly all of our materialistic possessions. Despite twenty years of marriage, I was learning that trust is fragile. It can easily be lost, and once lost, it's highly feasible it will never be regained.

I recalled that in my last counseling session with Rachel, we discussed my feelings of betrayal and my marriage. Rachel told me, "Betrayal happens in a marriage when there is infidelity, abuse, lies, lack of support, broken promises, secrets told, snooping, or stealing. It doesn't take all of these events, but certainly any one of them in combination with another can bring about a sense of betrayal. This, in turn, will result in feelings of anger, shock, hurt, disappointment, and disbelief."

As I sat listening, I mentally made note of how many of these factors were present in our lives as a result of my poor judgment. Rachel went on to say that, "The healing process is possible for both parties in a relationship if each is willing to:

Face their feelings;
Take care of themselves;
Communicate with each other;
Not be mistrustful of everyone;
Trust themselves;
Make a decision;
Let go of the anger;
Move on with their lives;
Grieve.

"If any step of this process is forgotten or ignored, the chances of a failed relationship increase dramatically."

In-depth discussions surrounding the understanding of each step carried into March 2002. For me, it was becoming painfully clear that Sara had become exhausted and was unsuccessful in coping with several of these processes. Communication had become nonexistent between us, and I believed that she had stopped trusting in herself, and her decision-making.

Sara carried the anger to the extreme and refused to let go of it, maintaining her in the role as a victim. Rachel said it was important to move on with life and not throw the past in the face of one's partner; Sara could not do this. Our marriage was not doing well; in reflection, our relationship had been deteriorating for quite some time.

Self-analysis revealed I was not exactly excelling at dealing with all of the steps either. I doubted almost every major decision within my personal life. And yet, at the same time, I had fallen on the sword, placing squarely on my own shoulders all of the responsibility for everyone's feelings of hurt, anger, disappointment, and pain. This alone had driven me into severe depression resulting in me not taking care of myself physically or mentally. I continued to be ill on a weekly basis, usually when I was alone in the evening worrying about the consequences yet to come. I had no insurance, and refused to go to the doctor for help.

Chapter 17

Work kept me busy, and 2002 was going faster than I had thought it would. Despite calling my attorney on a monthly basis, there was no news, which was good, according to him. Allen kept telling me the federal justice system moved extremely slow. Rachel felt I had progressed enough during our therapy sessions to reduce them to once a month. Sara and I had not improved our relationship; we were tolerant of each other and tried to communicate regularly about the kids.

I continued to talk with Joyce, which was still a major issue for Sara. I could not make her understand the loneliness and isolation I was feeling. My circle of friends had disappeared, leaving a void in my life regarding my need for companionship. Joyce filled that void through phone calls, e-mails, and infrequent face-to-face meetings. I had begged Sara to try and forgive me to help fill that void, but she refused. Numerous barriers kept us from renewing our commitment. I didn't know how long I could keep trying, only to get beat down again and again.

Working long hours, combined with softball in the evenings and week-ends, helped time pass quickly; however, I was not prepared for the phone call I received in late June 2002.

"Dan, this is Allen." My heart jumped to my throat and my hands immediately began to shake.

"I have been in contact with the U.S. Attorney and the Postal Inspctor's office. The anticipated charge being pursued is mail fraud, which is a class "D" felony. This is based on a check you sent to the claimant through the U.S. Postal Service meant to intentionally defraud the railroad. Now, in our past discussions, you have said that you wanted to cooperate fully with the investigation, so I have set up a series of meetings with the U.S. Postal Inspector and the FBI. Dan, are you listening?"

"Yes, so just exactly what does this mean?" As my immediate thought was that if I had taken the time to send all of the checks via FedEx, I would not be in this predicament.

"We will meet with the U.S. Attorney and the Postal Inspector, at her office, this Friday at 9:00 a.m. From what I understand, they want to interview you and enlist your help in the investigation into the McLloyd file. We can discuss this more in detail Friday. I want to meet with you about thirty minutes prior to our meeting with the Postal Inspector."

"O.K. How is this going to help me?"

"The more cooperative you are and assistance you provide into their ongoing investigation into the McLloyd file, the better you will look in front of a judge."

"O.K. Do I need to bring any paperwork or records?"

"No. If they need anything it will be requested through my office."

"Allen, thank you. I think."

"Dan, it will be fine. I'll see you on Friday."

I don't recall a week that went slower, other than the week I was terminated from the railroad. I was unproductive at work and my emotions ran rampant. Sleep came only in spurts and I couldn't eat enough Rolaids to calm my stomach.

When Friday finally came, I was a bundle of nerves. I dressed in a suit and tie, and despite having put on extra deodorant, was sweating profusely. All week long I tried to recall every detail of what I had said and done from the beginning of the case to the present. The drive to the office took about ten minutes. For the first time in a very long time, I prayed for composure, courage, and honesty

As we shook hands, Allen tried to reassure me. "Dan, calm down. There's no need to be this nervous. Let's find an office we can talk before the meeting begins."

"Lead the way."

"Dan, based on your discussion with them…"

"Who is 'them'?" I interrupted.

"The Postal Inspector and the FBI. As I was saying, based on your discussions, they may request a polygraph to prove your answers are truthful. The decision to cooperate to that extent will be completely up to you; I cannot tell you what to do, but we will cross that bridge at the end of today's discussions. Be honest and upfront, but answer only the questions they ask. Don't volunteer any more than what is needed to answer their questions. Do you understand?"

"Yes."

"Good. I will be beside you, and if any time you have a question or don't understand what they are asking, tell me."

"O.K."

"Let's go get the formal introductions over with and move on."

I followed Allen into a small conference room. The table held eight chairs; Allen and I were directed to sit at the far end of the table. Allen pointed across the table to a middle-aged woman, dressed in a navy, blue pantsuit with a white blouse, busy studying the file on the table in front of her.

"Dan, this is Melanie Demming, the lead investigator for the U.S. Postal inspector's Office handling your file."

Melanie looked directly into my eyes and offered her hand. "Dan, it's good to meet you, although I wish it were under different circumstances."

Shaking her hand, I replied, "Me too!"

"Mr. Grauer, sitting to my right is Mr. Ken Noland from the FBI. He will be sitting with us today during the interview."

As I stood and shook hands with Mr. Noland, Melanie addressed Allen. "Are we set to get started?"

"Mr. Grauer, before we get too far into this interview, do you understand that this interview is being recorded?"

"Yes."

"And is this being done with your permission and the permission of your attorney?"

"Yes, it is."

"Mr. Grauer, for the record, please state your full name, address, and birth date."

Following the formalities, I answered question after question surrounding my actions; exactly how I went about redirecting the expense funds, and all of the intricacy to cover up the fraudulent activities. Then the line of questioning began to take a different direction, one that concerned me greatly.

"Mr. Grauer, did your wife know what was going on all this time?"

"No."

"How can you explain the fact that she deposited some of the kickback checks received from McLloyd?"

"She did so under my direction."

I looked at Allen. "Allen, I need to take a break."

"Melanie, we have been at this for about an hour and a half. Let's take a thirty minute break."

"Fine."

Allen followed me outside into the parking lot.

"Allen, where in the hell are they headed with this?"

"They're fishing to see how much your wife knew about your activities."

"Why?"

"Dan, I have to be honest. They may very well seek to prosecute her as well, based upon what she knew."

"I cannot, nor will I, let that happen. I am responsible for this mess. I will not allow this, for the sake of my children. Me going to prison is one thing, but I will not allow my kids to also lose their mother."

"You have already told them you were responsible for what took place, but if your wife knew what was going on and participated in any way in defrauding the railroad, then she will be held accountable. Depending on how today goes, you may want to advise her to get an attorney."

"Allen, I can't let that happen!"

We walked back into the conference room. Melanie and Ken were already seated.

"Mr. Grauer, are you ready to resume?"

"Yes."

"Mr. Grauer, the time is 11:15 a.m. and I am turning on the tape recorder to resume our interview following a short break at your request. Now, Mr. Grauer, given all the extra money you suddenly had, wasn't it plausible that your wife knew something was wrong?"

"She confronted me at one time. I assured her that it was all on the up-and-up, and that McLloyd could do with his money whatever he wanted."

"But she didn't hesitate to spend the money, did she?"

"I have told you where the money went. I want to make it perfectly clear: my wife had nothing to do with my stupidity. Any money received was spent under my direction. I was the ONLY one in my family responsible for the fraudulent activity, period, end of story. I refuse to answer anymore questions about potential involvement of my wife, because there was none."

"Calm down, Mr. Grauer. We are just trying to cover all the bases."

"Fine."

"I think we are finished for today. Mr. Grauer, the time is 11:45 a.m., and I am turning off the tape recorder. Again, do you understand this entire interview was recorded and done so with your permission?"

"Yes."

I left the interview afraid. How could I prevent the prosecution of Sara? I could not, under any circumstances, allow that to happen for the sake of my kids.

In previous meetings with Allen, I had mentioned that Sara and I were separated. He asked if she would be in the courtroom as a show of support me, and I honestly didn't know the answer. In one of our more candid discussions, I asked Allen if divorce would protect Sara and the kids from any further investigation, or possible prosecution. Allen very honestly stated that this was not his area of expertise. Allen did concede that a divorce might create enough of a barrier to focus the investigation solely on me; however, he was also quick to say this should NOT be the sole reason for seeking a divorce. My relationship with Sara had been failing for some time so, if I needed to proceed with a divorce to protect Sara and the kids, then so be it.

In addition to everything else, Sara and I had agreed to sell the house in an attempt to get out from under some debt. I was already living in an apartment and she was willing to move into one. We had talked about all of the "stuff" we had accumulated over the years and agreed to have a garage sale to once again raise some money in an attempt to reduce some of the bill collection notices that had begun to stream in. I told Sara to sell everything that was mine that I had not already taken with me.

During the next three months, we held two garage sales. I sold everything associated with my past: tools, rifles, shotguns, fishing rods, golf clubs, mowers, and appliances – pretty much everything that I had purchased with tainted money. In the end we raised just over $1,600. I gave the money to Sara and told her to give me what she felt I was due; she kept all of it. I guess I should have expected that, but now I would have to turn to my family to help with legal expenses.

Discussions with my criminal attorney began to outline a picture of what to expect. Allen continued to reinforce his thoughts that based on what I had done, and in accordance with federal sentencing guidelines, I could realistically expect some prison time plus paying restitution for all I had taken. Just as in his first visit, he insisted that I plan for the worst, and if things went better than that, accepting less of a sentence could be dealt with easier than the acceptance of a harsher sentence. I laid it on the line regarding the dire straits my finances were in. Allen recommended that both Sara and I talk with a bankruptcy attorney.

We scheduled an appointment for the following week. The attorney we met with reviewed all of our financial records, statements, and debts, and then recommended that we file bankruptcy. Marc S. Ferro Jr., had practiced law in Nebraska for over twenty years. Marc was approximately 5'10", and balding, with only tuffs of hair over his ears. Years of legal research, and problem solving had taken its toll; he looked much older than his fifty-odd years. Confidence in his work and a supportive personality made his demeanor very pleasant in providing legal assistance to those that face the embarrassing reality that they could not control their finances. Marc left nothing to doubt when he discussed his assessment of the current situation, his fees, and his solution to the problem-at-hand. He was confident he could alleviate the onslaught of collection calls and nasty-grams we had almost every evening and weekend. The phone calls, both at home and work, gave Sara one more bullet in her gun that appeared to continually be aimed at my head. She did not lack in verbiage when telling me this was my fault, and I couldn't disagree. Although I still felt that if Sara would simply say she needed me, loved me, and wanted me to come home, we could work things out, and I would do so in a heartbeat.

I missed having the kids rumbling around, the sibling arguments and rivalries, but more than anything, I missed the hugs, kisses, and love that children unconditionally give. I was lonely with an extremely uncertain future, and the tidal waves of depression lasted longer and became more intense. Sara did occasionally let me keep K.C., our faithful and loyal black lab, but my current landlord didn't like dogs.

On Labor Day weekend 2002, I had both Alisha and K.C. staying with me. Joyce had come down for a visit on Saturday; she had met Alisha one time before, and they seemed to get along without a great deal of unnecessary tension. We had gone grocery shopping for dinner and had left K.C. in the basement apartment. Suddenly, my cell phone rang. "Dan, what the hell is that dog doing in my basement?"

"Diego, I asked you if I could keep K.C. for a couple of days and you didn't respond. He is housebroken and doesn't chew or destroy anything."

"I want him out of here NOW!" I could have heard him if the phone was still in my pocket.

"All right! We'll be there in just a minute and we can talk about this."

"What's wrong?" Alisha asked. I explained that I thought my landlord sounded drunk, and he was yelling about K.C. being in the apartment, and assured her everything would be fine.

We took about another thirty minutes to finish shopping, then headed back to the apartment. Diego was drunk, as I had suspected, and confronted me the minute I stepped into the entryway. He started yelling obscenities and began throwing a temper tantrum any nine-year-old would have been proud of. I listened to him yell, occasionally shaking my head in agreement, unable to get a word in. As he started to turn away, without warning, he grabbed my neck and laid a sucker punch on my chin, bringing tears to my eyes as I took a step back to catch myself. He threw another punch that landed squarely in the middle of my chest, taking my breath away. Although he was drunk, the punches still hurt.

I took another step back, debating whether or not to cut loose on this drunken bastard, or walk away. Joyce and my daughter were standing in the hallway and Alisha was yelling for Diego to stop. All I could think of was that I was already being charged with a felony, and an added assault would make things that much worse. Diego continued to call me everything except a white man, and his frustration only grew because I would not respond. He came at me one more time and I shoved him as hard as I could away. He stumbled back and I walked toward my apartment, with Joyce and Alisha leading the way.

Diego stayed in the main part of the house and didn't follow us into the apartment. More than physically hurt, my male ego and pride were bruised because my twelve-year-old daughter saw some guy get in two shots and I hadn't fought back. Joyce kept saying, repeatedly, "Dan, you did the right thing. Anything else would have made the situation much worse." Alisha looked at me with big, crocodile tears in her eyes. "Dad, are you O.K.?"

My jaw hurt and the imprint of a fist could clearly be seen on my chest, but other than that, physically I was fine. I sat down on the couch trying to clear my head. I had never seen Diego like this before, nor had he ever flown into such a rage; surely the presence of a dog in the apartment for a few hours hadn't done this. As we sat trying to analyze what had just taken place, there was a knock at the entrance to the apartment.

"LaVista Police! –OPEN THE DOOR!"

I looked at Joyce. "What the hell is this about?"

When I answered the door, two, uniformed police officers pushed their way into the apartment, demanding to know what was going on. I didn't have to say a word. Between Joyce and Alisha the scenario was given to the officers much better than if I had told the story.

"Mr. Grauer, Diego is the owner of this house, and he called us informing us that you had assaulted him." I did notice the officer referred to him as Diego and not Mr. Rodriguez; this alone was a pretty good indicator I was going to lose any attempted argument. I found out later that Diego was good friends with both of the responding officers.

"Take a close look at my chin and the bruise on my chest. Does it look like I assaulted that stupid bastard?"

"Well, Mr. Grauer, since he called this in and he is the owner of this residence, you have to leave."

"And just where the hell do you suggest I go since this is my place of residence also?"

"Do you have a friend or someone you can stay with for a day or two?"

For the first time the consequences truly took their toll. I had no one.

"Fine, give me a few minutes to pack some things and we'll go to a motel. Oh, by the way, tell that stupid asshole I just broke my lease agreement and will be moving out in the next thirty days."

"I will pass that along, Mr. Grauer. Please make sure you don't come back here until sometime tomorrow afternoon."

As I drove away, I looked in the rear-view mirror of my truck and saw both officers standing on the front porch, sharing a good chuckle with Diego.

Chapter 18

November 2002 found me living at the Sherwood Apartments on the east side of Council Bluffs, Iowa. They weren't anything extravagant, but did allow dogs, so that I could at least have K.C. once in awhile. I hated being further away from the kids and their activities, but did enjoy getting out from under the constant verbal battering of Sara, who had taken it upon herself to tell me just how much of a loser I was with every conversation.

The company I was working for as a career advisor began to show signs of failing. Clients that paid $3,500 to $4,000 for personal and professional career assistance began to feel they were not getting their money's worth. Handling forty-five to sixty clients at any one time did not allow sufficient time to dedicate to any one client, and juggling the amount of time spent trying to help them find careers was becoming extremely difficult. Additionally, many of them thought we were going to find them employment, and merely call them when they had a job; it didn't work that way. To successfully find a career took a commitment of time and effort on the part of everyone, not just the career assistance agency. Several clients had filed lawsuits and it was beginning to get ugly. I felt it was only a matter of time before the company went under.

Joyce's oldest daughter had a baby in November, and "grandma" spent less time with me, and more in the role she was needed. This added to my frustrations, although I understood that was how it should be. The holiday season brought with it a vicious cloud of depression and loneliness. My family wanted the kids and I to come down for Thanksgiving and Christmas. Trying to accommodate both Sara's family and mine resulted in the kids spending only a day with each side of the family. It was just as well. The love and support was all very visible, but so was the tension of our uncertain future. I did manage to get a Christmas tree up and decorated, dragging out the few ornaments Joyce had given me the previous year. As much as I tried to make the holiday special for the kids, I think they clearly saw through the façade.

Joyce did her very best to listen, comfort, and give advice on handling the various stages of my emotional distress, but I could sense she had issues of her own to deal with, and like many of us, was a better doctor than patient. We saw each other a couple of times per month, and talked almost daily on the phone. Keeping in contact with Joyce, I was able to keep control of the stress-induced irrational thoughts that often ran through my brain. While accepting responsibility for my actions, I also gave up the right to forgive myself and move past the barriers created by the consequences of my stupidity. Facing prison and a doubtful future with Sara was taking its toll, both mentally and physically.

In February 2003, I couldn't take any more of the tension at work. The extremely long hours and the lack of management to reinvest back into the company was causing a significant portion of the clientele to become upset with their lack of progress in finding the career of their choosing. I couldn't blame them. I knew when I drove to work that day I would be leaving, either immediately or at the end of the day, unemployed. I didn't need the additional stress; I had plenty of my own.

I informed my supervisor of my intentions on leaving and the concerns about where the business was heading; to my surprise she asked me to work through the end of the day. At 5:00 p.m. I packed my personal items in a cardboard box, said goodbye to my co-workers, and walked out the door.

I took a couple of days away from working just to unwind and relax. Monday of the following week I called a temporary employment agency and immediately accepted a position inputting medical billing for $10 per hour. I thought this might be what I needed, a mindless job based on production. When I was finished for the day I could leave without taking the stress of the job home. An uncertain future made it difficult to pursue permanent employment that would utilize my business skills, education, and experiences with any type of passion or drive. Each time I thought I found a new career position that would be the right fit, Allen Stallhaber's comments regarding potential prison time dampened my enthusiasm; however, I continued to look.

I had been inputting medical bills for just over a month when I received another call from Allen Stallhaber.

"Dan, this is Allen. I received a call from the U.S. Postal Inspector's office and they asked two things. First, would you be willing to take a polygraph test to validate the information you have provided them to date? Secondly, they want to have you get McLloyd on the phone and under their direction ask specific questions while being taped. I told them the decision was yours, but that we would talk about it."

"I don't have any problem doing that, but what do you think? Will it help in the long run?"

"I think if you do this the government will have to admit in open court that you did everything within your power to assist in the investigation. This would set well with a judge."

"O.K., how soon do they want to do this?"

"Friday, if you can arrange it."

"Go ahead and set it up."

"One more thing Dan. We need to talk about my charges. You have paid about $12,000 to date. We agreed to $15,000. Can you work on that as well?"

"Allen, are you telling me that eight meetings with you and we're averaging about one phone call per month has used up $12,000?"

"Dan, we made an agreement of $15,000 up front, I just need you to work on getting that paid off."

"O.K., I'll give my brother a call. Do you have any idea when this is going to come to a head? The stress of not knowing is keeping me from seeking any kind of permanent employment and is a real source of added anxiety."

"In talking with the U.S. Prosecutor in charge of your case, he is swamped with numerous criminal cases far more serious than yours. Last time we spoke he anticipated it would be late fall, October or November."

"Allen, if you were in my shoes, would you accept a permanent job if it became available?"

"Yes, and here's why. I have told you to prepare for some prison time, and I believe that will hold true, but the possibility does exist, slim though it may be, that you might get off with restitution and probation."

"O.K., thanks. I guess I'll talk to you on Friday. Do we need to meet beforehand as we did last time?"

"I don't think so. I am comfortable with how you handle yourself. I will leave you a message with the time."

"O.K."

I hated getting calls from Allen on a Monday. The remainder of the week was filled with anxiety due to my runaway imagination. I know my medical billing data entry production was down that week, but I really didn't care. The temp agency was able to provide me some tips on companies and corporations that were looking for permanent employees in risk management. I kept my resume up-to-date and continued to send out five to ten per week.

On Friday, I put on my suit and tie, and drove to the Postal Inspector's office, arriving fifteen minutes early for the scheduled 10:00 a.m. meeting. I waited in the parking lot for Allen's arrival. He pulled in with about five minutes to spare. We shook hands and walked together toward the main entrance.

"They're going to try and call McLloyd first. Listen to what Melanie Demming tells you regarding the type of information she wants elicited from McLloyd. He is not going to know the phone line is tapped."

"O.K."

"Following the phone call, they will conduct the polygraph test. It's not admissible in court, but I think they want to validate as much of what you have told them as they can."

"O.K."

"Are you nervous?"

"Is there any reason I SHOULDN'T BE?"

"Relax, you'll do fine."

We walked in the door and were immediately greeted by Melanie Demming. We followed her into the same conference room my initial interview had been conducted. At one end of the table was a phone hooked up to some type of machine with an extra earpiece. I assumed this allowed them to tape the conversation and listen in at the same time.

"Dan, have a seat in front of the telephone," Melanie instructed, pointing to the chair where the phone was located. Allen sat next to me; Melanie sat in front of the machine with the extra earpiece.

"Dan," she began, "we're going to call McLloyd. I want you to tell him you have been contacted by the FBI and the Postal Inspector's office regarding the money he received from the railroad. We have looked into all of his financial accounts and already have the information on file so you're not lying to him. Next, you have told us that it was McLloyd's idea for the "kickbacks;" you need to revisit the past and try to get him to admit that this was his idea. You also need to get him to say that despite the fact you wanted to stop, he continued to send you receipts and demand money. Take your time. Try to make this as natural as possible without tipping our hand. Can you do that?"

"I will try."

Melanie handed me the telephone receiver and dialed, started the tape machine, and picked up the extra earpiece so she could listen to the conversation.

"McLloyd residence!"

"Lance, Dan Grauer. How are you doing?"

"Been awhile since we talked Dan. What's going on?"

"Well, I have some bad news. I've been contacted by the FBI and the U.S. Postal Inspector asking me about the money you received from the railroad."

Silence.

"I told them that I was in charge of the claim and authorized all payments that were made to you. I just wanted to give you a heads-up that they were looking."

"And. . . ?"

"Lance, do you remember when all this started and we discussed how this would work? I told you that if this was what you wanted to do, I wouldn't stop you, remember?"

"Dan, that was so long ago. I really don't remember."

"Well, do you remember when you called me to tell me you were sending me some receipts that NEEDED to be reimbursed?"

"I don't think I said it quite that way, did I?"

It was like a slap in the face. Suddenly, I realized that this supposed good friend was hanging my ass out to dry. Like a fox, he wasn't going to remember anything he had said, and if something went down, it was me that would hang. I looked at Melanie Demming who sat expressionless and was writing notes in addition to listening.

"Lance, if these folks come back for another visit, just what the hell do you want me to tell them?" Melanie passed me a note telling me to calm down and not get mad.

"I don't know what you should say, Dan."

"Lance, I trusted you on this. Each time you sent me receipts, I accepted your word that they were somehow related to ongoing medical treatment and problems you were having. They were, weren't they?"

"I still can't raise my arm above shoulder height and the pain is ongoing."

Shit, he's not going to answer anything I ask in a manner that would incriminate him in anyway. I was on my own. About the same time, I got another note from Melanie that said to "End it."

"Well, Lance, I don't know what I will tell them if they come calling again."

"Dan, you were in charge of the claim. Any check I received from you, I assumed was done with your authority. I don't know what else to say."

"You don't have to say anything else, Lance."

"Dan, let me know if they contact you again."

"Yeah sure, no problem," and I hung up the phone.

Melanie was the first to speak. "Well, he turned out to be some friend, huh? He didn't do you any favors."

"Yeah, I know. Now what?"

"Dan, you did the best you could. McLloyd was smart enough not to answer any question directly or in a manner that would bring him into the picture. We will continue our investigation. The polygraph machine is set up in another office; follow me and we'll get this wrapped up."

Allen stood and told me he needed to leave for a court appointment. He shook my hand and once again offered words of encouragement. I followed Melanie to another office on the other side of the building. We stepped into a small, maybe 10' x 10' office, painted the same bright white as every room in the building. Melanie introduced me to the polygraph technician and told me to have a chair in front of the desk. On the desk was a machine about the size of a small fax machine. It had graph paper on it with heat-marking instruments attached, just like on TV. The operator was busy fine-tuning the machine.

Melanie said, "Dan, when you're done, we'll talk for a few minutes and then you'll be free to leave."

"O.K.," I said, sitting in the chair to which I was directed. Melanie left and closed the door.

The operator came to my side of the desk and began hooking up a blood pressure type of cuff to my arm, then he put a respiration sensor around my waist. He explained, step-by-step, what he was doing and why, but I was so nervous I don't think I heard much of anything. Finally, he stepped around to the other side of the desk and sat down.

"Mr. Grauer, I need to ask you some sample questions to calibrate the machine to your responses. Throughout the test, I will ask simple questions that don't require a great deal of explanation. To get started I will ask three questions; answer them truthfully and honestly. I will then ask the same questions again; this time, however, I want you to lie and give false answers. After I have calibrated the machine, we will get started."

"O.K."

"Mr. Grauer, how many children do you have?"

"Three."

"Mr. Grauer, how old are you?"

"Forty-three."

"Mr. Grauer, how many times have you been married?"

"Once."

The operator made some adjustments to the machine and then said, "O.K., Mr. Grauer, I am going to ask you the same questions again and I want you to lie."

My answers this time were: fourteen, sixty-eight, and four. Again, the operator made some adjustments and was finally ready to proceed. For the next hour I was asked the same questions in simple format that I had been asked in every interview to date. I took my time answering each question and gave serious thought to each. I noticed that many of the questions were repeated in a different manner. I tried to make sure I would give the same answer. About an hour and ten minutes into the testing, the operator looked up and said, "Mr. Grauer, I have only a few more questions, then we'll be done."

"Did your wife know that what was taking place was illegal?"

I think my heart skipped a beat. I knew that I had to remain calm and keep my respiration as steady as possible. I paused for a moment, took a deep breath, and said, "No."

"Did she ever encourage you to keep the money coming in?"

"No."

"Did she ever cash the checks received from McLloyd without your direction?"

"No."

"Did she help spend any of the illegal monies obtained?"

"No."

"Are you sure, Mr. Grauer?"

"Yes."

"Mr. Grauer, do you ever lie?"

"Yes."

"Mr. Grauer, are you lying about the participation of your wife?"

"No."

I could feel the sweat running down my back and I knew that I had failed the last portion of the polygraph, but I was going to try and protect Sara at all cost.

"O.K., Mr. Grauer, I think we're done here. Let me take the results, visit with Ms. Demming, then I will come back." He stepped out and headed up the hallway.

Roughly twenty minutes later he returned, opened the door, and said, "Mr. Grauer, Ms. Demming would like a word with you before you leave. Please come with me."

We walked into the same conference room I had been in during the three previous meetings. Melanie Demming was studying the list of questions and comparing them to the resulting lines on the polygraph sheet.

The polygraph technician began the conversation.

"Mr. Grauer, it looks like you have told the truth for the most part. There are a few areas that are questionable, but I cannot out-and-out say you are lying." He continued, "Mr. Grauer, you admitted to lying. Just what else do you lie about?"

Once again, I took a deep breath and contemplated my answer.

"Well, it always made me uncomfortable to tell my kids that Santa Claus and the Easter Bunny were real, and I have cheated on my golf score, haven't you?" I glance at Melanie Demming and thought for a moment I saw a smile, almost.

"Mr. Grauer, this isn't about me or Ms. Demming. The answers you gave at the end of the testing were questionable at best."

"Well, given what I have done, if you knew how mad my wife is, I assure you it would make you nervous to talk about her too!"

Once again I thought I saw a slight smile on Melanie Demming. She looked at me and said, "Dan, that's all I have. You're free to go. I will write up my reports and submit them to the U.S. Prosecutor and your attorney. I am going to note that you have fully cooperated in every aspect that I have asked. This will most likely be the last time we meet. I am going to ask that you not contact McLloyd in any way, shape, or form as that investigation is still ongoing. Do you understand?"

"Yes, Ma'am."

"You're free to leave."

I stood, walked out of her office and the building like it was on fire. I was glad to have been finished with my part of the investigation, but still extremely nervous about the possibility of Sara facing prosecution as well. Melanie Demming had said she was going to talk with Allen about the results. I made a mental note to call him at some point during the next week to see if she had done so.

Chapter 19

On the following Friday I called Allen to see if he had received the report from Melanie. He said she had called him and given a verbal report, but he had not yet received the written version. Allen said she felt that I was covering for what knowledge Sara had regarding the fraud, but that she didn't have any direct evidence and was not going to pursue that avenue. She told him her report would state that I was fully cooperative with her investigation. They were still investigating McLloyd and he reminded me to have no contact with him. Her opinion was that I had tried to help someone and had gotten in over my head, which led to extremely poor decision-making and illegal activity. She thought I was truthful in providing the information she asked for in her investigation. Then Allen said, "Dan, she said you seemed like an intelligent and likeable guy who knows right from wrong and seems to have some sense about values. What she couldn't figure out was why?"

As a lump formed in my throat, I replied, "I don't have the answer for that either, Allen. I wish I did because then maybe I could have find some peace with all that has taken place."

"Dan, I will call you when I hear more. If you have any questions, you are always welcome to call me. By the way, your brother took care of my fees, so don't worry about it."

"When did he do that?"

"He called me this week. Since he is an attorney, I gave him a complete assessment of the case, and where I felt we were headed. I like him, Dan, and you have to know he is worried for you."

I hung up the phone without a response.

Through our therapists, and with their input, Sara and I had several discussions about divorce and how each of us could make the best of the split for ourselves and for our children. I agreed to use one attorney chosen by Sara. I would give her everything except what I had already taken, pay her attorney's fees, and whatever child support the court deemed appropriate. I didn't have a time frame that would be up to Sara and her attorney. I knew that I would need to call both Allen and Marc and let them know what had been decided.

Allen said he had a feeling this was coming by the number of visits Sara attended with me. Marc said that we need to meet with him because he could not represent just one of us as it would be a conflict of interest. I told him I would try to reach Sara and we would set up an appointment sometime during the next couple of weeks.

The middle of April the house finally sold. It had actually only been on the market for a few weeks. The sale didn't quite cover what we owed on it, but we also couldn't afford to keep making payments on the house. Once again, my older brother, Dave, came to the rescue and provided the needed $3,500 to get us out from under the house payments; I had no clue how I was going to pay him back. Sara had moved into an apartment complex near the house and put a good deal of the furnishings in storage. The apartment she had chosen would not take pets so I was going to get K.C. on a permanent basis, at least for a while. It would be nice to be greeted when I came home, even it was K.C..

Joyce stayed with me a couple times a month. She continued providing insight on what I might expect from Sara and the kids, especially the emotions they would be feeling when I would eventually be indicted and possibly go to prison. I really appreciated the openness and honesty with which she addressed my questions, although she frustrated me at times; I wanted someone to feel sorry for me and Joyce simply refused to do that. She continued to support Sara's attitude, providing me with an understanding in what it was like to be a victim because she, herself, had walked in those shoes. Her feedback and suggestions on handling the emotional roller coaster the kids would be riding was valuable in keeping them close to me as a father. I have to admit that I simply enjoyed her companionship.

I finally caught a break in late April. The hundreds of resumes and follow-up phone calls produced an interview with Continental Insurance Company as a Risk Management Trainer. I was ecstatic; I knew that if I could get an interview, I could convince anyone willing to give me a chance that I would be an asset. I did, however, think it was strange that I had plenty of confidence in my abilities as a professional, but had lost a majority of my self-esteem as a man and father. I hoped and prayed I could recapture the latter.

The interview went extremely well. Amanda, the departmental manager, and I clicked from the first introductions, and I was offered the position starting on June 1. I would be working with a team of five trainers, all specializing in the training of specific types of insurance coverage from dental to life. The first few weeks would be spent learning the curriculum, on-the-job training, and eventually training in disability and life insurance coverage. The salary was a good starting pay and the benefits were exceptional. I was excited.

The first month of my new career demanded a steep learning curve in the specifics involved in the Continental Insurance policies that pertained to disability claims and their applicable business operations. It felt good to use my brain again for something other than a hat rack. My co-workers were professional, and knowledgeable, yet friendly. I was given the latitude to learn at my own pace, yet the autonomy to begin the development and implementation of new training programs. Continental was an exceptional company with exceptional employees, and yet, I dared not get attached to anyone or any part of the job because I also knew my past would eventually come to haunt me. However, for the first time, in a very long time, I actually enjoyed getting up in the morning and heading off to work. Each day was filled with new challenges and presented the opportunity to improve some aspect of the business operations.

I just knew that my feelings of contentment were too good to be true and, sure enough, the third week into my new job, I received a letter from Sara's divorce attorney. The petition for the dissolution of our marriage had been filed in Sarpy County District Court and was signed by Sara on March 23, 2003. As I read through the petition, I thought I was prepared for everything: the child custody, visitation, the $863 per month child support and the division of the debt, that was until I reached the date for which the hearing had been set. I don't know how Sara managed it or even whether or not it was intentional, but the hearing was set for July 18---my birthday. Even my birthday would no longer be a celebration; instead, the day a twenty-year marriage ended. Well, I guess my birthday is as good as any day to remind me of my stupidity from the previous five years.

The remainder of June seemed to fly by. I was given the latitude to develop some checks and balances in the claims payment processes within Continental. Having utilized my past experiences, I wanted to make sure no other corporation would fall prey to someone who could take advantage of the system as I had done at the railroad. Additionally, I began to develop back and neck injury protocols for use in handling disability claims based on my years of claims research and development within the transportation industry. This work was encouraged and welcomed with open arms; I felt like I was accomplishing something good again.

July 4 fell on a Friday and Joyce was going to spend the weekend with me. From our past conversations I had learned that she truly enjoyed a good fireworks show. Ralston, Nebraska held a fantastic Independence Day parade that entertained both young and old alike, and the Lakeview Golf Course, also in Ralston, put on one of the state's best fireworks displays. When I told Joyce about the parade and fireworks events, she was worse than a little kid at Christmas. She suggested we invite all of our children to watch the fireworks. I thought that was as good of a time as any for all of them to meet. Joyce's daughters were going to meet us at the Ralston parade at 11:00 a.m. The parade itself wouldn't end until around 2:30 p.m. The crowd tripled the population of small-town Ralston for a few hours. It always seemed to be sweltering hot so it was important to pick out a good spot under a shade tree early in the morning or suffer the consequences of the sun.

The parade exceeded everyone's expectations. Jaylon, Joyce's grandchild, came away with plenty of candy and prizes. Everyone was worn out from the heat and the excitement of the parade. We headed back to my apartment for a nap before the fireworks display that evening.

I was beginning to get a little bit nervous about all the kids being together. Joyce's kids were all survivalists, but not by choice. They each had distinguishing characteristics and personality traits, but they all exhibited a sturdy sense of personal identity. I believe this allowed them to think independently and choose a course separate from that of the herd; they weren't much for rules and could bend the truth when needed to keep them out of trouble. This, in turn, led to limited social interaction skills.

Johanna, the oldest, was married with one child and pregnant with a second due in late July. She was very reluctant to accept the relationship

Joyce and I had developed. Johanna still idolized her father, despite his misgivings, because as the oldest, she, like many daughters, could get about anything she wanted from her father. She left the nest early, but not by choice. Jo made some judgmental errors in choosing friends and habits, but like many young women was forced to quickly mature and change given the responsibility of children. I viewed her relationship with Joyce as one that had been tremendously rocky in the past and was just now beginning to heal. Johanna came across as extremely intelligent and imaginative in her thinking. She could rationalize just about anything, and "think outside the box" for solutions to ideas that I had never even considered.

Emmylee, the second child, was truly independent and serious about her interactions with family and friends. She appeared extremely mature, more so than her age. Joyce had said that Emmylee was a key factor in her survival over the past years. In my limited exposure to Emmy, she never ceased to amaze me with her rational thinking and brilliant idealism. I worried, however, that Emmy had been forced to mature too quickly and had become a partner for Joyce during her struggles. I felt that having put Emmy on a pedestal equal to a parent in the sharing of both family and financial responsibilities had left Emmy missing out on much of the fun found in just being a teenager. I quickly reminded myself that I was in no position to judge anyone's ability to parent.

Montana was the youngest. He was very bright and knowledgeable, but had such a carefree life style, he chose not apply any of the above, at least not right now. I truly admired his ability to just shrug off his problems. His circle of friends was limited to those that had the same buoyant thought processes. Montana was indeed a "hippie" caught in the wrong time period.

All of the kids were extremely protective of their mom. I was determined that they never forget their father, nor the good memories they shared. They were extremely individualistic, but would pull together and defend one another like madmen when necessary. The biggest difference I noted among them was that in their modes of forced survival: Johanna could bend, limit, or just ignore the truth if it was to her benefit; Emmylee would only do so if it would keep her out of trouble; and Montana was just brutally honest with a "take me as I am" attitude. They were all good kids who deserved a much better hand than they had been dealt.

My biggest concern was that Joyce's children and my children came from opposite sides of the street. My kids had been spoon-fed, spoiled, and given pretty much anything they needed and wanted. Joyce's kids on the other hand had to earn everything they had. I just didn't know how the personalities would mesh.

At about 7:00 p.m. we started to round everyone up and head out the door. I hoped to find a place to park relatively close to the fireworks, but far enough away that we wouldn't have to crane our necks upward to enjoy the show. Joyce was already dancing around, displaying an excited frenzy that any nine-year old would have been proud. It made me smile to watch her.

As we drove south along 72nd street near the golf course, Joyce pointed to a place where vehicles were starting to congregate behind the Dairy Queen. She thought this would be the perfect spot to watch the fireworks, so we pulled off the street and backed my truck onto the grass. We then called everyone's cell phone to let them know where we were located. Alisha was with us; Johanna, Emmylee, Tiffany and Montana were all going to meet us.

The fireworks began promptly at 10:00 p.m. Applause broke out among the crowd on several occasions in appreciation of the beauty and elegance of the colors and imagery surrounding the small skyward explosions. Joyce was fascinated, her hand over her mouth holding in the "ooos" and "ahs" to the point of tears. I quickly made a mental note of the simple pleasure Joyce derived from a fireworks display and promised myself to make this a tradition if our fate was to be together in the future.

As for our children, they pretty much hung out within their own little family cliques. The minimal interaction that was visible was courteous, but extremely cautious of one another. All in all, the night went really well and I believe everyone had a good time.

It had been several weeks since I had become nauseated to the point of vomiting, but as July 18 closed in, so did the attacks. Rolaids and Tums minimized the ache, but rarely lessened the frequency. I could be doubled over in gut-wrenching pain. I had lost approximately twenty pounds in the last six months, which made my clothes fit much better, but I could never recommend to anyone this particular diet plan. I took July 17 and 18 as vacation from work to mentally and physically prepare for the hearing.

I arrived at the Sarpy County courthouse at about 9:30 a.m. to meet with Sara and her attorney and go over the petition. A part of me wanted to thank Sara for such a wonderful birthday gift, but I couldn't bring myself to say anything; she sat on a bench near the doorway to the courtroom and wouldn't even look up. Her attorney walked toward me as I entered the hallway, presented me with the petition, and told me what questions the judge would likely ask. I glanced through the petition, taking note of the visitation, which was every other weekend and every other holiday. The debt was to be split by mutual agreement. I had tried to take on a majority of those financial obligations. The only real objection I had was the calculation of child support: Sara had provided our IRS records for the last year, which included withdrawals from retirements and investments. They had calculated my annual income to be $53,000 when in reality it was $40,000. The amount of child support being sought was $1,238 per month. There was no way I could afford that. Her attorney said this could be amended and didn't see any problem with changing it, provided I could provide proof of my income. Based on what I had told her, the child support guidelines for the state of Nebraska dictated that I would pay $864 per month for Tiffany and Alisha. This would be automatically withheld from each paycheck. The last item that caught my attention was the $692 attorney fee assigned to me for payment.

I lowered the petition as Sara's attorney indicated it was time to go into the courtroom. The entire hearing took less than twenty minutes; twenty years to get where we were and twenty minutes to end it. For some reason I found that amazing. I left the courthouse wanting to go directly to the bar, but knowing that if I did, someone would be pouring me into bed. So, instead I just went home and turned into a couch potato.

Chapter 20

Joyce always seemed to provide a motivational and spiritual lift, whether due to a simple conversation or a visit with homemade apple pie in hand. However, day-to-day, it seemed my attitude would change, one day reaching a new high and the next a new low. The antidepressant medication I was on seemed to make the peaks and valleys at least tolerable. One constant seemed to be that my ongoing stomach pain and nausea did not subside after the last bout in July. I began to have even more indigestion and always felt tired. It was early August when one particular episode of stomach pain and nausea lasted well over four hours that I finally decided to drive myself to the emergency room.

Following the usual lengthy wait to see a doctor, I was finally brought back to an exam room. Another twenty plus minutes went by and I was actually starting to feel a little better. I debated whether or not just to leave, but decided that since I finally had some insurance, I would stick it out and see if there was a problem. The doctor finally made it into the exam room and began the usual line of questioning.

"Mr. Grauer, tell me about the stomach pain and nausea you are experiencing. Let's start with the pain. On a scale of one to ten, with one being mild and ten being excruciating, how would you rank your pain?"

"Well, right now, about four; an hour ago, a seven or eight."

"How long has this been going on?"

"On and off, for a very long time."

"Long time as in weeks, months, or years?"

"I was terminated from my job in January 2001. I have had episodes on-and-off since that time."

"Why didn't you see a doctor?"

"No insurance until my most recent employment beginning June of this year."

"When you say nausea, does this cause you to get sick to your stomach or is it more just indigestion?"

"Both. There have been times when I would vomit until I got the dry heaves and other times when it was really bad heartburn and indigestion, but it always seemed to subside and get better."

"Are you vomiting any blood?"

"Occasionally, but not very often that I have noticed."

"Do you have any difficulty swallowing?"

"No, not until today when this particular episode seemed really harsh."

"What other symptoms are you having?"

"I just seem really tired, as in dragging, not necessarily sleepy. Does that make sense?"

"Let's see, you're on antidepressants, high blood pressure, and high cholesterol medication, correct?"

"Yes."

"Do you take any other medications?"

"Just ibuprofen to help control ongoing back ache resulting from a back surgery in 1991."

"How much alcohol do you consume in a week?"

"Lately, none. I have never been a heavy partier. I would never drink more than a few beers a week."

"Is there anything that makes the nausea better or worse?"

"Not really. Eating will sometimes irritate things, but I haven't been able to eat much lately."

"Have you had any significant weight loss?"

"I don't know what you mean by significant. I have lost about twenty pounds over the past six months, but honestly could stand to lose another thirty."

"Mr. Grauer, go ahead and lay back on the exam table."

The doctor listened to my stomach with his stethoscope, and then began a two-handed physical exam working his way around the abdomen applying pressure. At one particular point he hit a tender spot that about made me jump right off the exam table. He stopped and paused, looked me in the eyes, and said, "Dan, I know that was uncomfortable, but I need to do that area one more time, O.K.?"

I shook my head yes. With as much tenderness as possible, he began to probe one more time, this time bringing tears to my eyes.

"I'd like to go ahead and take some blood and get a chest x-ray."

"O.K. Why when you hit that one area did it hurt so bad?"

"Well, I'm not sure yet. It's obviously not your appendix since you don't have it any more. We may be looking at an ulcer or some other things. Let me get some blood drawn, then we'll talk again."

It seemed as though it took a very long time for the lab technician to come in and draw blood. This was followed by another wait to get a chest x-ray. I looked at my watch. I had been in the emergency room for about two hours, but it certainly seemed much longer.

The doctor finally came back into the room, looking down at the chart as he walked.

"Mr. Grauer, your red blood count is low and that concerns me a little. During the physical examination I'm certain I felt what may be a lump on the stomach in the area where all of the pain seemed to be radiating." He stopped and stared at the chart once again. "Here's what I think," he said, looking over the top of his glasses, "I am going to give you some antacid and some phenergan suppositories for the nausea. Your chest x-ray looks fine. I want you to follow up with your family physician in the next two to three days. There may be a few more tests that your physician will want to do."

"O.K."

He stood up and closed the chart. "The nurse will be right in with discharge instructions. Make sure you follow up with your physician."

On the way out of the emergency room I took a big swig of antacid from the white bottle, folded the prescription, and put it in my pocket. I was feeling a little better so there was no hurry on getting the prescription filled, and my physician was in West Omaha, so if I continued to feel better, there would be no hurry there either.

Chapter 21

Physically, I felt that I had begun to improve. I continued to lose some weight and eating was not the major undertaking as it had been the past. I was truly enjoying work, developing risk management programs and policies. I had not heard from my attorney during the last two months and assumed that this was a good thing; however, lurking in the back of mind was a tormentor of what the future might hold. Sleep never came easily and when extra time was at hand, anxiety and panic could take control of my mind. The games my mind could play were overwhelming and exhausting, both physically and mentally on a bad day.

Toward the end of September, Emmylee, Joyce's youngest daughter, was talking about moving to Omaha. She felt that her life had become stagnate in the South Sioux City area and that she needed a change of scenery. She had been deeply hurt in a relationship and was working "dead-end" type of work.

I told both Emmylee and Joyce that she was welcome to move into the second bedroom of my apartment. She could find employment and get on her feet then move forward. I could see in Emmylee's eyes that this was an appealing offer, but I left the decision strictly up to her. The issue was one of trust. Of all of Joyce's children, Emmylee was the least critical of our relationship, and I believe she was beginning to see some positive changes in her mother. Joyce seemed to laugh and smile more. She actually began to dream again and worry less.

I am not exactly sure what took place in South Sioux City on September 28, 2003, but my phone rang at approximately 9:30 p.m.

"Dan, this is Emmylee."

"What's up? Is everything all right?" She had never called me before unless it was to talk with her mother, and Joyce wasn't with me.

"I want to take you up on your offer to move in."

"Cool! When do you want to do that?"

"TONIGHT! I'm packing as we speak and will be leaving here around 11:30 p.m. My family is being so stupid, my job sucks, my life sucks, and I just can't take it anymore so I am leaving."

"Have you talked with your mom?"

"My whole family sucks! I've had it and I'm leaving."

Well, what was I going to do at that point? I was about to have a roommate. "I'll leave the door open and the light on, just like Motel 6."

"Thank you. I'll try to be quiet when I come in."

"O.K., be careful driving down that late."

"I will."

As I hung up the phone, I thought to myself, *Oh, My God! What have you just gotten yourself into Daniel?*

At about 2:00 a.m. K.C. went berserk. He jumped off my bed, and ran down the hallway growling and barking like his life depended on it. He raised such a ruckus I about peed my pants. Then it dawned on me that Emmylee was "home" and I had forgotten to unlock the apartment door. K.C. was going to rip apart whoever was on the other side of that door and he was letting the world know.

I stumbled out of bed and wobbled to the door. "Emmylee, is that you?"

"No, it's the Maytag repairman. Yes, it's me. Open the door, I got my hands full!"

Well, let the excitement begin. I opened the door and Emmylee walked right past me like she was part owner. I briefly showed her where the bedroom and her bathroom were located, made sure she could handle all she brought with her, then I went back to bed, shut the door, and went to sleep, sort of.

I lay awake for quite sometime, listening as Emmylee seemed to make trip after trip in and out of the apartment. I almost laughed out loud at her no nonsense personality. I was going to enjoy the company. Little did I know then, that Emmylee and I would sit up for hours when neither one of us could sleep, having intense discussions and debates on issues that I hadn't thought about in years. She became very special to me; I grew to appreciate her intelligence, knowledge, and openness during our late night "talks."

Just as July 18 would never be a birthday celebration again, October 17 became another milestone haunting my past. Sara and I were married on October 17, 1981. On October 17, 2003, my phone rang with the dreaded news I had known would come someday.

"Dan, this is Allen. How are you doing?"

"Well, to be honest, I was having a good day until I heard your voice."

"We have a court date for the indictment."

"O.K., what does that mean?"

"We have to appear before Judge Brandon E. Michaels. He is a good and fair man; I think he is a good judge for this case."

"I don't know about that......"

"Why do you say that?"

"We had numerous personal injury claims that involved Judge Michaels, I have a tremendous amount of respect for the man, but he is another acquaintance that I am not real thrilled about facing."

"Dan, we could have done a lot worse."

"O.K., so what does this all entail?"

"We will be present before Judge Michaels and he will make sure you understand everything that has transpired to date. He'll ask if I have informed you of all possibilities including the plea, the plea agreement, and potential consequences. Once he is comfortable that you have a good understanding of the charges and the process, he will ask you to plead "guilty" or "not guilty." You will answer "guilty." You will be released on what is called a personal recognizance bond and be ordered to report for a pretrial evaluation. He will also set a sentencing date."

"Am I going to be arrested and handcuffed?"

"No, you have demonstrated there is no need for that. You will be required to complete some paperwork through the U.S. Marshal's office following the hearing, but you will be free up until the sentencing date. Even then, Judge Michaels will recommend a date that you will be required to report to any incarceration facility. As we have discussed, it will most likely be Yankton, South Dakota."

"Do you think we can get the sentencing date postponed until after my daughter, Tiffany, graduates high school in May?"

"Honestly, probably not, but we can ask."

My heart had begun beating so hard I could almost hear it. Indicted in November, sentenced in February, and most likely in prison by who knows when. I could see that this was going to be a wonderful holiday season and I would most likely miss my daughter's high school graduation. 2004 was not going to be a good year.

"What do I need to do to get ready for the November 4 hearing?"

"Nothing. Keep working and carrying on with your life just as you have for the past several months."

I hung up the phone and just sat at my desk, too numb to move. I needed to inform my boss of these dates. I had informed them of what had taken place in my past, but I was not sure how they would accept the current situation. After a few minutes I stood up and headed for the human resources department, unsure if I would have a job when I walked away or not.

I met with the Director of human resources. He had attended one of my training presentations regarding low back injuries and was commenting on how much he had learned. I was looking at his face, not really hearing what he said.

Finally, I heard, "Dan, what can I do for you?"

"Do you remember when I hired on we discussed the legal troubles I was having that resulted from my previous employment?"

"Yes, why?"

"There has been a new development I need to make you aware of. Charges are going to be filed and an indictment handed out on November 4."

"O.K., so does that mean you're going to be sentenced to anything serious?"

"I don't know yet. I know that I can't afford any more legal fees, so I am going to plead guilty and accept whatever consequences may come of it."

"Are you going to be sentenced for anything?"

"Not that I know of, at least not yet."

"Come back and talk to me when we have to cross that bridge."

"O.K., I just wanted to keep you apprised of what was happening".

"I appreciate you doing that and I expect you to continue keeping us updated."

As I stood and shook hands on the way out of his office, I said, "Thank you. I hope you continue to take care of all of your employees as you would your family; that's part of what makes this company so great to work for."

My anxiety increased dramatically over the next eighteen days, with every imaginable scenario running through my mind, with no answers and truly unimaginable consequences leaving me sitting straight up in bed, a cold sweat running down my back.

Physically, the stomach pain and nausea were winning the battle. I tried to eat and stay hydrated, but it seemed a losing battle. I had to make it to November 4 and would go to the doctor at some point in time after that.

November 4 found me in my best suit to go to the courthouse at 7:00 a.m. My hearing was not scheduled until 10:00 a.m.; I would meet with Allen at about 9:30 a.m. to discuss any questions regarding procedure and expectations. The drive to the Federal courthouse was almost fatal. My imagination was running wild and I became so distracted that twice I pulled in front of other motorists. One of those close calls resulted in an extremely angry commuter slamming on his brakes and steering his skidding vehicle to the shoulder and off the highway. Needless to say, I didn't have to be able to read lips in order to understand what was being yelled at me.

I was extremely scared and alone! As I finally arrived in the courthouse parking lot and shut off the car, I looked down at my trembling hands and folded them together for the first time, in a very long time, and had a long discussion with God. I wanted Him to know that from the moment I made the choice to straighten out this mess to this very moment, I had felt alone. I was angry with Him about how I felt physically and mentally, was full of self-pity, and was feeling sorry for myself.

Once again, as He had done many times, He gave me a reminder that my burdens were not as bad as I thought. As I opened the car door, I glanced toward Dodge Street in time to see a cold, hungry, seemingly homeless man making his way down the street, stopping to pick through garbage cans and slapping his arms against the bitter, north wind. The man's sweater was worn out, pants were full of holes, and he had only one shoe. I suddenly felt ashamed.

I was ashamed that it seemed as though the only time I turned to Him for guidance, discernment, and wisdom was when I was in trouble. I paused, silently thanking Him for my blessings.

Judge Michaels sat majestically behind the bench in his black robe. I watched as he silently read through the file in front of him, occasionally shaking his head. The disappointment he must have felt toward me was easily seen in his face. He hadn't said a word, but given the look on his face, I began, once again, to choke back tears.

"Mr. Grauer, as you stand before the court today, do you understand the charges that have been filed against you?"

"Yes, your Honor, I do."

"And, Mr. Grauer, has your attorney fully explained these charges, their meaning, and the potential consequences?"

"Yes, your Honor, he has."

"Mr. Grauer, how do you plead?"

My knees began to sag; I couldn't have worked my way out of a wet paper bag. I felt so weak.

"Guilty, your Honor."

"Mr. Grauer, I accept your plea of guilty. You will report to the U.S. Probation Office for the preparation of a presentence investigative report. You will also present to the U.S. Marshal's office for processing. Sentencing will be scheduled for February 17, 2004."

I felt Allen's hand on my shoulder.

"Dan, we're done. You need to go downstairs to the U.S. Marshal's office. They will take your photograph and fingerprints. Then you need to go to the U.S. Probation office and make an appointment for a presentence investigation. You will be assigned a probation officer and have to report to them, monthly most likely."

"O.K.........Allen, I. . ."

"Dan, it's going to be all right. I want to meet with you yet this week and discuss the sentencing."

"O.K., I'll call you."

I felt his hand at my elbow as he slowly guided me out of the courtroom. It was as though I couldn't make it on my own, and truth be known, that may have been true.

At the U.S. Marshal's office, I was fingerprinted and photographed, just like on TV, a frontal photo holding my future prison number and a profile photo holding the same. They fingerprinted each finger and took also my palm print. Number 18951047 was imbedded into my brain. I was still wiping the ink off my hands when I entered the U.S. Probation office. I told the receptionist behind the glass that I was here as to begin the presentence investigative process.

Minutes later the door to the main offices opened and a lady, by the name of Jackie Baker, stepped out.

"Mr. Grauer?"

"Yes."

"Come with me. If you have some time we can get a majority of this out of the way now."

I followed her down a narrow hallway, lined with offices and generic paintings on the walls. We didn't walk far when she turned left into a small office.

"Have a seat, Mr. Grauer."

"O.K."

"Let me explain what is going to happen over the next few months. I am going to conduct what is called a presentence investigation. This will consist of getting as much information as possible from you, about you, and about what led up to the current charges filed against you. I will verify and validate as much of the information you give me as I can. Has your attorney discussed with you the U.S. federal sentencing guidelines?"

"Yes."

"It is my job to talk with you, your attorney, and the prosecutor and make a sentencing recommendation to Judge Michaels based on the results of my investigation. I will give Judge Michaels, you, and your attorney a copy of my report. Your attorney can dispute anything in the report that is felt to be inaccurate. From this point forward, you will consider yourself on presentence probation and we will meet monthly. Do you understand?"

"Yes."

Two hours later, I had retold my story of the last two years. Ms. Baker asked questions as we talked about income, family, relationships, and my current physical and mental health. I was open and honest. At this point in my life, I had done all I could humanly do to correct what I had done wrong.

I looked at my watch as I climbed the stairs to the main level of the courthouse. I had been at the courthouse for about four hours and I felt like I had been run over by a Mack truck. As I walked out the front door, my emotions began another pounding wave. All I could think of was that this was certainly going to be some merry f _ __ing Christmas.......

Chapter 22

The stress was taking its toll. My attitude had become horrible towards everyone in my life. I had trouble focusing at work, concentrating on projects, due dates, and paying attention to detail in general. I felt as though I could sleep sixteen of twenty-four hours if I could have. I was late getting to work and could find just about any excuse not to go to work at all. My eating habits were extreme, one day eating, "the ass end out of a bear, fur and all," as my Grandpa would say, and other days I rarely ate or drank. I just didn't care! My mind played games with me continuously, allowing me to envision only the most negative consequences imaginable each day that came closer to February 17.

Veteran's Day was particularly difficult. I had been in the United States Air Force and was proud of my military career, but my mind kept telling me that a true veteran would not be in this situation.

Throughout the entire week, my stomach convulsed in pain, and nausea swept through my body. As much as I tried, and as much as I wanted, sleep was not to be had. I had lost control of my life and my emotions. I truly began to feel as though I was trapped deep inside a dark cave with not even a sliver of light; worse yet, tomorrow would only be the same. Thoughts of dying became prevalent.

I only wanted the pain to stop and to be able to go to sleep. I don't recall exactly all that happened. I was on the phone with Joyce one minute and the next I was incoherent. I was told that had it not been for Joyce calling Emmylee and having her check to see how I was feeling, I might not be alive. In an attempt to sleep, I had taken numerous Tylenol PM and other medications I had around the house. Emmylee had called Joyce back on the phone and stayed with me, yelling and slapping me to keep me conscious. When Joyce arrived, she took me to the emergency room, chewing my ass the entire way there.

In the emergency room, I was given a charcoal mixture to drink. I can remember the nurse saying, "Here, drink this. Then plan on sleeping by the toilet for the next several hours." I don't know what combination of medications was administered, but I do know that sitting on the toilet and vomiting in an emesis basin for hours on end was not my idea of fun on a Friday night.

I was admitted to the psychiatric ward for evaluation. Joyce visited me on Saturday, still extremely upset. Nothing I could say was going to convince her that I had just wanted some sleep. I begged her not to tell my kids; I did not want them to know what I had done. Joyce had already told me that Emmylee was angry; guess I couldn't blame her.

An entire battery of psychological tests was administered during the next twenty-four hours. An extensive interview with a psychiatrist was also part of the mental evaluation, followed by ongoing outpatient therapy. I was dismissed on Sunday afternoon and returned to my apartment. Outpatient psychological therapy was scheduled, as was an entire battery of medical testing for the ongoing stomach pain and nausea.

I was feeling a little better both physically and mentally. I was getting medical bills from past treatment and, not wanting to saddle anyone with my debt if sentenced to prison, I ignored all the follow-up recommendations. I had already been a burden to my family and was determined not to continue to embarrass them any further, regardless of the cost.

However, that wouldn't be the case. An episode of vomiting blood, trembling, and severe stomach pain resulted in seeing the doctor again on November 17. A thorough medical exam, to include history, physical exam, and blood tests, was ordered. As the doctor pressed on my abdomen, as the emergency room doctor had done in August, a tender spot brought instantaneous pain and tears to my eyes. This time the doctor stepped away, made some notes on the chart, and turned back around to face me.

"Dan, we may be dealing with something potentially serious here. As part of the blood tests I am going to ask them to check for a chemical substance that sometimes shows up in the blood stream called C.E.A.. This chemical marker tends to show up about 50 percent of the time in people who have stomach cancer. I am not saying at this point that's what you have, but we do need to do some more tests. I also want to schedule what's called a barium swallow. This will be done on an outpatient basis in radiology. Let's get this done as quickly as possible."

"Isn't it possible that this could simply be an ulcer or some type of stomach irritation?"

"Yes, but for as long as this has been going on, I think there's more. We'll know more after the barium swallow. I want you to get this done tomorrow. You can't eat or drink anything for about six to eight hours prior to the test. I am going to send you down to the x-ray department to get this scheduled."

"How long does the test take?"

"The entire test takes about an hour. You'll change into a hospital gown and get an injection to relax the muscles of the digestive system. You'll then be given a white chalky type of liquid to drink. As the barium passes through the digestive system, it is followed by a series of x-rays that will show any growths or ulcers. They will explain more to you in radiology. Take this slip and go down there immediately."

I didn't like the emphasis on the word "immediately," but followed the doctor's orders and went to radiology. The staff was kind and professional, but pretty much repeated what my doctor had said would take place, asking that I be at the hospital by 7:30 a.m. the next morning.

I arrived at the hospital about 7:15 a.m. After completing all the necessary paperwork and releases, I changed into a hospital gown and was escorted into the x-ray room, was given the injection to relax my muscles, and directed to a type of couch. The technician explained that after I swallowed the barium, the couch could be tipped into different positions during the test to cause the barium to flow wherever necessary so that the x-ray could identify any potential problems.

True to their word, about an hour later I was getting dressed. The radiology technician said the doctor would call me with the results in twenty-four to forty-eight hours, and reviewed all of the standard dos and don'ts following this type of testing. I tried to pry additional information out of the technician, but she was professional and would only say the doctor would call me.

Within a day, my phone rang. "Dan, this is Mary. I'm a nurse at Alegent Health Physician's Clinic. The doctor would like to talk with you if you have a minute."

"Sure."

"Not over the phone, but if you could swing by late this afternoon about 4:30 p.m., he would like to visit with you about your test results."

"I can do that," already thinking that this couldn't be good.

I arrived at the doctor's office about 4:15 p.m.. With anxiety and fear building all afternoon, my shirt was damp from sweat. Finally, I was called back to an exam room where the doctor was waiting, thumbing through the chart.

"Dan, I have the results from the blood work and the barium swallow. The chemical marker we spoke about (C.E.A.) is present and somewhat elevated. The barium swallow has identified a growth in one of the outer stomach quadrants. Dan, these two combined is a good indicator that you may have stomach cancer. We won't know for sure until we do further testing, but we this needs to be done sooner than later."

I am not sure I heard anything more than the word "cancer." What else could go wrong? Hadn't I been through enough?

"Dan, if our tests are confirmed, stomach cancer can be beaten with an aggressive treatment plan. We need to set up a laparoscopy to biopsy the growth sight. Dan, are you listening to me?"

"Sorry, I need you to know that I can't deal with this right now. I am going to tell you straight up, I'm not going to do anything until after Christmas."

"Dan, we need to get these tests done to know what we are dealing with."

"Doc, I just told you. I'm not going to do anything until after Christmas. If you want to schedule something then fine; if not, fine."

"Dan, do you realize the seriousness of. . ."

"I said, not 'till after Christmas,'" cutting him off mid-sentence.

"FINE. I can only advise you to get this immediately." Looking at the calendar, he pointed to the week of December 29. "How about December 30? Will that work?"

"Fine, just not right now."

"I will have our office call you on the 29 with the necessary instructions. Until then, keep taking the antacid and I would suggest you stay on as bland a diet as you can. If the pain gets worse, you need to call me. Dan, do you hear what I'm saying?"

I shook my head yes, but I had already made up my mind that from now on, things would happen on my time frame.

Chapter 23

I decided not to tell anyone; they didn't need to know, at least not right now. Though Joyce was an integral part of my life, I wasn't sure about our future. Joyce had asked me to go to her parent's house in Osceola, Nebraska this upcoming weekend. Her father had been diagnosed with lung cancer and had been going through chemotherapy and radiation. She had enough on her mind without worrying about me.

We arrived at the Jacobsen residence just before noon. I'm not sure who was more nervous, Joyce or me. I had told Joyce not to hide anything about my past from her family; either they simply would accept me for who I was, or they would not. Joyce pulled no punches, hiding nothing in her telephone discussions with her parents. I felt that given her past relationship, I was in for an uphill battle of prejudice

The house was a small, ranch-style home with a single attached garage. Some flowers with their final blooms decorated the front of the house. With just a glance, anyone could see this house was cared for by someone who enjoyed the outdoors, and with a passion for nature. As we stepped onto the front porch, the door opened. In the doorway stood an elderly woman, about 5'4" tall, not overweight but no longer petite, gray hair, and wrinkles etched into her face. Powerful eyes hidden behind gold-rimmed glasses still held the youthful spark of a woman used to having things her own way. She came across as someone who got right to the point, with no hesitation. As the screen door opened, she hugged Joyce, then stood in front of me. "We've heard a lot about you," she challenged, as I began to step inside the house.

"Is that good or bad?" I asked.

Staring me directly in the eyes, "That remains to be seen, young man."

"Well, it looks like I have some work to do then, doesn't it?"

"Yes, I believe you do," she said, as she pivoted on one heel and walked toward the living room, leaving me standing in the doorway.

Joyce had already made herself at home and had walked across the living room floor to give her dad a hug. I took four slow steps into the house and stood at the edge of the living room. Just like the outside of the house, the inside was well cared for: decorated with ceramic farm animals, floral pictures, and gifts from children decorating almost every available space. On one side of the living room was a white "L" shaped couch with a coffee table in front of it. On the other was a greenish colored couch and matching recliner. In the recliner was Glen Jacobsen.

I could see that he was a proud man who had worked hard all of his life for everything he had. His facial features were set deep into a weathered face with tired eyes. They didn't carry the sparkle and enthusiasm of the man I knew that had built all that surrounded him and provided for his family. He looked to be only a fraction of what had once been an extremely physically powerful man. His pride, however, was still going strong; he stood giving me a firm handshake as I stepped in front of this worn-out, gentle giant. Without a word he returned to his chair and began sizing me up, as he must have every man that crossed his path throughout the years

Joyce was the "garage sale" queen. I think she could spot a garage sale sign from half-a-mile away with both eyes closed. As we drove toward her parents she commented that she might ask her mom to hit a few of them. I asked her if her dad got out of the house much since undergoing chemotherapy; she said he had not, so I began formulating a plan.

It took Joyce all of about three minutes of being inside her parent's home to ask her mom about going to some garage sales. Idelle looked at me to see if I was going to panic. I merely looked over at Glen and asked, "When's the last time you've been for ride in that truck of yours sitting out front?"

"It's been awhile and it needs driven."

"Well, throw on a shirt, and let's take a drive. You can show me the county roads you maintained for so many years and where you used to live."

He looked me in the eye for what seemed like forever, but then a grin crossed his face and he said, "Why not, but you have to drive."

154

"I think I can handle that."

For the next two hours we drove on miles of country roads. Glen knew every farmer in the county. We pulled into the homestead where he had lived. He opened the door to get out, so I quickly did the same, almost sprinting around the truck to make sure Glen didn't fall. I grabbed the back of his arm as he began to walk, and at first I thought he was going to pull away, but he didn't. He just gave directions on which way to walk and talked about how everything used to be: what building stood where, where he kept the cattle and the chickens, and how much he missed farming.

I felt comfortable with Glen. I asked questions about farming, irrigation systems, cattle, road maintenance, and his tour of duty in the war. He seemed to appreciate someone taking the time to listen. I think in the short time we spent together, I had learned more about Glen than even his kids knew. The man was a walking history book of local knowledge and stories.

We talked about his health and his concerns about the future. He discussed the chemotherapy and radiation treatments, and swore he wouldn't do it again. He told me he was ready anytime the Lord saw fit to take him, and, in the same breath, made me pledge to not tell his family what I had heard. The conviction, courage, and faith with which he spoke made me realize I had a long way to go.

Glen asked about my past and listened intently as I spoke candidly of my stupidity and lack of judgment. Occasionally, he would shake his head in agreement saying, "Go on." I told him about almost everything that occurred. We talked about my recent diagnosis and I asked that he not share this with his family. He seemed to understand my asking him to keep this secret.

Given all the energy and enthusiasm Glen had exhibited during our afternoon excursion, he tired just as quickly. I could see that he was struggling and needed to rest, so we headed back to the house. In the short time we spent together, my respect for Glen Jacobsen soared. In my estimation, Glen was the type of man that true heroes were made of, and anyone should have been proud to have him as a father.

Soon we pulled the truck back into the yard, underneath the pine tree, right where it belonged. Glen told me to leave the keys in it as he struggled with his door.

"Glen, let me help you with that." I could see that his mind was willing, but not his body. He sat back and waited for me to assist him into the house. Once inside and in his chair, it was only a matter of minutes and he was snoring peacefully. I wondered how long he could fool his family; he was losing the battle quickly.

In typical Joyce fashion, when hitting garage sales, what began as a couple of garage sales turned about three and half hours. The two ladies came traipsing in the door laughing and giggling about where they had been and what they had seen, though neither had bought anything.

About 4:30 p.m. Joyce announced that it was time to leave. Glen was still snoozing, and it looked as though Idelle would be soon, so we passed out hugs and headed back toward Council Bluffs.

Joyce immediately asked about my afternoon. She couldn't believe Glen went on a drive with me; she seemed fascinated to learn all that I had heard. Glen had told his family he was a tank driver in the Army, so when I told her that he spent a good deal of his tour behind a machine gun mounted on a jeep, guarding enemy prisoners, she was astounded. He had never mentioned that, but then, she admitted, no one had ever asked. Joyce wanted to hear everything we had talked about and began to cry when I told her about our stop at the home place. She had a really good afternoon with her mom, and I had an awesome day with her dad; the visit was well worth the drive.

This would be the last drive in my Chevy Silverado pickup. The lease was up and I was turning it in on Monday. I had purchased a 1989 Honda Accord to get me through February 4 The engine ran smoothly and got great gas mileage so I wasn't going to complain. Besides, $1,500 spread out over a couple of months was all I could afford.

Chapter 24

Thanksgiving arrived quickly. My parents invited Sara and the kids as usual. Ryan was home from college. He was frustrated with both of us, as his perception of our family was being shattered, one step at a time. Tiffany and Alisha had begun to accept the separation, although I think they both secretly wished we could somehow reconcile our differences. While Sara agreed to see my family for Thanksgiving, she refused to ride in the same vehicle with me. Sara, Tiffany, Ryan, and Alisha would ride down together; I would be down later the same day.

My family tried to act as though nothing was wrong, treating Sara with the utmost respect and kindness. I expected nothing less, and still, by doing so, felt a little betrayed. Mom and dad went out of their way to insure my children knew they were loved by my family. They also made it known that no matter what the future held, they would be there.

Mom, despite having a stroke at age sixty-five, and having only roughly 15 percent use of her right side, cooked up a storm. It never ceased to amaze me what she could do with a little determination and one good arm. Despite the obvious lack of communication between Sara and I, this holiday would be no different than those of past years: too much to eat, too many family stories, and not enough time to enjoy it all. I do have to admit, sleeping in separate beds away from Sara in my parent's house was strange, but it felt right.

Following dinner Sunday evening, the karma within the family began to change. It was time to return to the grind of everyday life and reality.

Ryan decided to ride home with me and the girls elected to follow us back to Omaha. Ryan pulled no punches, sharing his frustrations and anger during the ride home. I respected him for doing so, but at the same time, I wanted to explain my reasoning for what was happening. I elected just to listen. Just south of Lincoln, Nebraska Ryan suddenly yelled, "Dad, DEER"!

It was too late; as if I was living by Murphy's Law, I hit the deer head-on, regaining control of the car and managing to power it to the shoulder. My heart was pounding hard as I looked to make sure Ryan was all right. He was still staring out the windshield, as though he was waiting for something else to happen.

"Ryan, you O.K.?"

"I think so…"

"Let's get out and see how much damage was done."

Sara and the girls had managed to miss the deer and had pulled in behind us, along the shoulder of the highway. Ryan and I began to walk around the vehicle, sizing up the damage. Sara, Tiffany, and Alisha joined us in the inspection. It was immediately obvious the car would not be driveable and the damage was significant. Basically, the front of the car had been pushed back into the engine about two feet. I had elected not to insure the car because it was older and I was only going to be driving it for a few months anyway.

I couldn't believe this was happening. I think every cuss word known to man came out of my mouth and probably a few never before heard. My kids looked at me in utter astonishment; they had never before seen me this angry. After a few minutes, I finally calmed down enough to look at Sara and ask if our AAA account was still active. Upon confirmation that it was, I called them on my cell phone. It would be about forty-five minutes before they could get there. I also called the Lancaster County sheriff's office to make a police report. I had no idea how I was going to pay for the damage or for that matter get back and forth to work. Just one more brick on what seemed like an already overloaded wheelbarrow.

Once the car was securely locked behind the tow truck and directions given to the truck driver, we crammed into one vehicle and continued our journey. The remainder of the drive was extremely quiet. Everyone looked out their separate window, seemingly caught up in their own little world.

Monday morning, I called into work and took a day of vacation, not yet having devised a plan for transportation. I talked with mom and dad and told them of our excursion home. I think they were as frustrated as I was at my lack of luck. Shortly before noon my phone rang. It was my little brother, Dennis, calling to "check on me." It soon became apparent that he had talked to mom and dad because, once again, my family bailed me out of a jam. He offered to not only pay for the damage to the car to make it useable, but also help me pay for a rental car for a few days. I was so overwhelmed that I couldn't even bring myself to say, "Thank you."

During the next four days my car was rebuilt using used parts. Joyce hadn't run away despite all that she knew about me and physically I was feeling a little better. While my nerves were frazzled, I was no longer ready to throw in the towel. I returned to work and spent some time with the corporate medical director discussing issues pertaining to my stomach cancer. He was very optimistic based on what the doctor had shared with me; however, like my doctor, recommended having the laparoscopy done immediately.

I had put the finishing touches on several training programs for the claims representatives, and had presented them with positive feedback that made me feel as though I had indeed accomplished something during this entire fiasco. Joyce continued her unconditional support and what seemed to be an unlimited amount of patience with me. Standing back and trying to evaluate our relationship from her perspective, I wasn't sure I would have stuck around as long as she had, but I'm glad she did.

Her dad's health continued to deteriorate. In a conversation with our corporate medical director about Glen, he put his hand on my shoulder, looked me in the eyes, and said, "Tell Joyce to spend as much time with him as she can now." Based on this we decided to make another trip to Osceola the following weekend. It was December 12, and the wind was so strong that I needed to keep both hands on the steering wheel to stay in our lane. When we arrived, most of Joyce's family was there, which she had neglected to tell me.

I met her brother, Russell, her sisters, Charmayne and Holly, and their spouses. Each seemed like they were representative of the typical American family. They appeared to love one another and their children. Each of them seemed to be people possessing strong moral values, wanting only the best for their children, and wanting their children to know that God existed. The one common factor I did observe was that all of them failed to recognize just how close Glen was to the end.

Idelle, just like my mother, felt the need to cook and feed the entire herd. Glen was weak, content to sit in the recliner and listen to the surrounding conversations. I played the "1000 Question" game with Joyce's siblings, being as honest and open as I dared. I don't know where I got the courage, maybe it came from a Higher Power. Suddenly, with no warning, I decided to make an announcement.

"Glen and Idelle, you know that Joyce has been a part of my life for about two years. She knows my past and I hers. We have kept no secrets from each other and I believe that God has brought us together for a reason. Neither Joyce, nor I, know what that reason is yet; however, I need you to hear this."

Seated on the couch next to Glen's chair, I looked into his eyes and, without hesitation, said, "Glen, if it is God's will, may I have your permission to continue to care for Joyce and make her my life partner at whatever point in the future is best for us? I don't think either of us knows when that time might or will come, but if it's God's will, then I would like your blessing as well."

He sat up straight and looked me in the eye; his hand slowly came off the armrest of the chair to rest on top of my hand. One big crocodile tear rolled down his cheek as he said, "Dan, no one has ever asked my permission before. I believe that things will turn out just fine in your future, and yes, I would like you to take good care of my daughter."

"Glen, if it is meant to be, then that's a promise I will keep."

I'm not sure who was more surprised by the conversation: Joyce, her siblings, or me. When I looked away from Glen, Joyce and her sisters were crying, and Idelle's embedded frown had turned into a smile. Russell stepped up and gave me a bear hug and then, just as suddenly, everyone began to laugh.

Later, on the drive home, Joyce cried again without giving any explanation for the tears. I hoped they were tears of comfort, but I was relatively certain reality was setting in regarding her father. For the first time, in quite awhile, she spoke about all the good memories of her childhood: growing up, her family, and especially of her father. I was content to listen.

On December 19, Joyce received a phone call from her sister, Charmayne. Glen had been admitted and was not doing well. Charmayne was a nurse and at her urging, we made another trip to see Glen. On Saturday morning when we arrived at his hospital room, Glen was scarcely recognizable. He had lost even more weight, was mostly incoherent, and had lost control of his bodily functions. My past medical experience told me that Glen would be in the hands of the Master in twenty-four to forty-eight hours.

Joyce was in shock. She had never before seen her father like this. She wasn't sure what to say or what to do. Finally, she stepped in close, grabbed his hand, and rubbed his cheek with the back of her other hand. I looked in her eyes and watched as all the words she wished she would have said to her now failing dad came out in tears.

After about ten minutes, Joyce, Charmayne, and Idelle left the room to get some air. I stayed with Glen, holding his hand, and keeping his dry lips damp with a cool wet washcloth. I talked with him as if he could hear me and understand every word. At one point, I knew he heard me. "Glen," I said, "When the Lord comes calling, it's O.K. to go home. Take his hand and let go of the pain and suffering."

His head rolled toward me and he looked into my eyes. With no hesitation he said, "I know, and I'm ready." Glen quickly drifted back into his own world; one , which I prayed, was better than ours. Glen's family each spent time with him, reminiscing. About 4:00 p.m., Joyce walked up to me and said she was ready to head back toward Council Bluffs. I asked her multiple times if that is what she really wanted; I thought she should stay with her family. Joyce said she couldn't take anymore of the sadness and needed to leave.

We had been back in my apartment and in bed for less than thirty minutes when the call came. Glen had died. Joyce sobbed, rocking back and forth for over an hour with no consolation to be had. I gave her two Naprosyn and two Tylenol PM. Finally, about 2:00 a.m., she fell asleep for a couple of hours.

I had not planned on taking off the entire week of Christmas; I didn't have that much vacation. I only hoped work would understand. I would call my supervisor later and explain. If they didn't, then I would take unpaid leave.

Sunday morning found us on the road, headed back to Osceola to lay Glen to rest. The family was gathering to make the arrangements and it was important that Joyce be there. I was sad for Joyce and her family, but happy that Glen's suffering had ended. He was indeed ready for his journey home; I wondered if I could be as strong and courageous when facing my future.

The funeral and burial would be December 23, with a veteran's service at the Lutheran church where Glen and Idelle had been lifelong members

I believe most of the Osceola inhabitants, and a majority of the county, attended the funeral. Glen was a popular man, well liked and held in high regard within the community. Eulogies told of his past, his accomplishments, and what were his dreams for his family; many tears were shed and memories relived during the process of "letting go." He was a good man, and I was certain would not be forgotten. I had made a promise to Glen and I had every intention of keeping my word. I only hoped I would be strong enough, both physically and emotionally, to do so, but then it wasn't in my hands, was it?

Following the funeral and lunch, Joyce once again announced she was ready to go home. During the last few days I had noted that while "love" could be seen between family members, they didn't display the closeness I shared with my brothers. Despite feeling like the family's "black sheep," my brothers and I worked to keep track of one another and what was happening in our lives. I would talk with my parents weekly while Joyce was content to do so monthly, maybe. I called my brothers once every couple of weeks, Joyce every couple of months. It made me sad that it took a funeral for a family get-together and I knew that Joyce's family wasn't the only one in that boat.

The drive home was quiet. Joyce, I know, was contemplating her past, memories of her father, and what could have and should have been said, but wasn't. I was content to let her dream and reminisce. I also knew that with Christmas and New Year's fast approaching, the next few weeks would be extremely difficult for her and her family. I would encourage her to spend time with her children, siblings, and mom.

Chapter 25

Normally, I always look forward to Christmas. The act of giving, the lights, and I believe the one time of year when ninety-eight percent of the people are somewhat happy. I have to admit that I do go a little bit overboard. Christmas music is fair game anytime after July 1. Christmas lights and decorations must be up the week after Thanksgiving, and the Christmas tree up and fully trimmed by the first week of December.

None of that was going to happen this year. Following our return from Glen's funeral, I managed to get a Christmas tree put up, stockings on the wall for all of the kids, including Joyce's, and I even had some gifts under the tree. I had strung some lights on the apartment balcony, but it just wasn't the same. I was used to having so many Christmas lights up that airplanes could mistake my house for runway landing lights. I had to remember that's not what Christmas is all about anyway; maybe I still had that lesson to learn.

Sara and I had separate Christmas celebrations for our children. Joyce's children were still extremely uncomfortable around mine, so we had a separate Christmas for them. We needed to plan some time for Joyce's mother and her family. My parents wanted to have a couple of days for a Christmas celebration, which included their standard invitation to Sara.

This holiday season would be about trying to keep all the family members happy and spending just a smidgen of quality time with everyone. Christmas fell on a Thursday, so, with my remaining vacation, I would be off work through January 4, and most of it would be spent in a car traveling. This was the one time in my life when I wished I could have bypassed the Christmas season.

I had all but forgotten about the promised laparoscopy to follow up on my cancer diagnosis until my phone rang right at 8:00 a.m., the morning of December 29. I had continued to take the antacids and nausea medication. I tried to control the pain instead of letting the pain control me, and, quite frankly, I had been so busy that I simply spaced it off.

The nurse explained that this was an outpatient procedure, but would be performed under general anesthetic. Through one or more small incisions, the surgeon would insert a camera and a light into the abdomen allowing visualization of the suspected tissues, take a biopsy, and the pathology lab would determine staging if it turned out to be cancer. The procedure itself would take approximately thirty minutes to an hour; however, due to the general anesthetic, I needed to plan on a minimum of four hours from arrival to departure. I was to be at the hospital by 6:30 a.m., and report to Outpatient Surgery. The doctor will visit with me before I left, but any test results would be shared in a follow-up appointment scheduled within a day or two. I was not to eat or drink anything after midnight, and to forgo all medications for that morning.

For some unknown reason, it didn't dawn on me that this would be done under general anesthesia. I still didn't want to tell my parents. Telling my brothers was out of the question because they had already done so much, and I wasn't about to tell Joyce with what she had just experienced with her father.

I picked up the phone and called Sara.

"Sara, it's Dan. I have a favor to ask."

"What?"

"I know our relationship isn't worth a damn to you right now, but I am going to ask anyway."

"What do you want. I am busy."

"Sara, the most recent diagnosis with all the stomach problems I've had is potentially stomach cancer. Tomorrow at 7:00 a.m., I'm having a laparoscopy procedure to determine a more accurate diagnosis. They have to knock me out to do it. I guess I am a little scared and didn't want to wake up by myself. Would you be there?"

After a long pause, "I can't take off work without any notice."

"Sara, I don't want anyone else to know what's going on right now. Don't you think I have caused enough trauma within our families. Please?"

"I can't get off work."

"O.K.. Tiffany is a senior and out of school. Can I have her there?"

"I don't think that would be appropriate, do you?"

"Sara, I don't want to beg. I am a bit scared and would like someone there when I wake up. Is that so unreasonable?"

"Well, then why don't you ask Joyce?" and she hung up the phone.

I stared at the receiver. I couldn't seem to grasp what had just taken place. Sara's anger was so intense that twenty years of marriage meant nothing. I couldn't help but think that if the roles were reversed, I would have been there for her, simply out courtesy. As I hung up the phone, I thought to myself, *Screw it, what happens, happens. If I don't wake up, then so be it.*

I didn't sleep; my mind raced with every possible scenario of what could go wrong. I wanted to call and talk with Joyce, but I couldn't. I knew that if I did I would ask her to be with me, and given all that she had just gone through with her father, I just couldn't. I wanted to call mom and dad, or my brothers, but I had already wreaked enough havoc into their lives without adding to the chaos. I just needed to step up to the plate and get this done.

I finally got up and showered at about 4:00 a.m. I couldn't have anything to eat or drink so I turned on TV, trying to distract myself. At 6:00 a.m., I decided that maybe if I went to the hospital early, I might get in and out quicker. The first question I was asked was, "Who is going to drive you home?"

"I am."

"Well, don't you have anyone that you want to be here?"

"Not today."

"Mr. Grauer, you understand that we'll have to keep you in recovery longer until we are certain that you can safely leave on your own. The doctor may even want to keep you overnight."

"I understand."

The paperwork was extensive and detailed. I took my time reading through all of the releases and permissions. Signing the understanding of risk was difficult, especially when considering the last sentence. "As with any surgery the risk of death may occur. . ." Well, I hoped not. I was intrigued that I was giving the doctor permission to make any medical decision deemed necessary to facilitate the quality of the health care being provided.

Just as I was signing the last form, the doctor stepped into the room.

"Dan, the nurse will be coming in shortly to give you a shot to relax you. Do you understand what is taking place this morning, and do you have any questions?"

"If you find a problem area or, for lack of better words, 'a bad spot,' will you remove it while you are there?"

"It will depend on the size of the area. Generally, with a laparoscopy we are limited to diagnosis, but if the area is small enough, we may remove it, yes."

"And what if the area is larger than what can be handled during the laparoscopy?"

"Dan, you're jumping way ahead of where we need to be. Let's take this one step at a time."

The last thing I remember was the medication being put into my IV that was supposed to relax me. It worked. Next thing I knew, a nurse was standing over me telling me it was time to wake up. I would be in outpatient recovery for most of the day, or until the nurses made sure everything was working properly again. The procedure went just as the doctor had described. I had two laparoscopic holes in my belly less than an inch long; each had a couple of stitches showing. My stomach however felt like someone hit me with a two-by-four.

After about an hour of being awake the doctor stopped by. "Dan, we found a tumor about the size of a nickel. I removed as much I safely could, and I believe we got most, if not all if it. This will be sent to the lab for confirmation, but I believe you are in the very early stages of stomach cancer. First, let me explain how we classify your cancer."

"Hold on a minute, doc. You just said you couldn't conclusively tell if I had stomach cancer until the lab results came back, and yet you're now going to tell me how to classify my cancer?"

"Dan, listen to me. I have been doing this for a good number of years. What I saw, I can tell you with 99 percent certainty is cancerous. What I am trying to tell you is that we caught this in the very early stages and I would classify this as stage 1b or (T2, N0, M0). Let me explain what all of this means: "TNM" stands for Tumor, Node, and Metastasis. This allows us to describe the size of the primary tumor, whether there are lymph nodes with cancer cells in them, and whether the cancer has spread to a different part of the body."

I was trying really hard to listen, but I wasn't ready to hear that I had cancer. I was starting to get really scared, and wished I would have had someone with me.

"Are you hearing what I am telling you?"

"Kind of. I am trying really hard to listen, but focusing is a problem."

"I understand and we'll go over all of this several times during the up-coming weeks. Try to focus. I believe we have caught this early enough that there are no cancer cells in the lymph nodes, but I do believe the cancer has grown into the muscle of the stomach wall. The good news is that about only 6 percent of the people diagnosed with stomach cancer are diagnosed this early. Your prognosis is really good."

"Define really good."

"With stage 1b and stage 2 stomach cancer, generally speaking, just over 40 percant of the people diagnosed will survive greater than five years. Beyond five years of no recurring cancer cells, the medical commu-nity will generally accept this as a cure, although this is not always the case."

"So, what you're telling me is that I have between a 50 percent and 60 percent chance of beating this."

"What I am telling you is that we caught this very early and you are in a better position to beat this than a vast majority of the people diagnosed with stomach cancer. I want you to relax at least a couple of more hours and I will try to check back on you before you leave."

I was encouraged to eat ice chips, drink liquids, and was eventually told that I wasn't going to leave until I could get up, walk to the bathroom, and pee. The sooner all this occurred, the sooner I could leave.

The doctor stopped by with discharge instructions about four hours later.

"Dan, I'd like to see you next Monday, January 5. I'm going to have the nurse make an appointment before you leave. Have you been able to get up and ambulate?"

"Yes."

"What about urination? Any trouble?"

"No."

"I'd like you to stay off work at least two days. You have a sedentary job, correct?"

"Yes, it's mostly a desk job. If I feel like going to work can I go? I'd rather be there than sitting around home thinking about what you've told me."

"Use good judgment. If you can get around with minimal pain and without difficulty, you can go back, but limit yourself on what you do. How much pain are you in? You're going to have a good amount of stomach soreness due to the manipulation of the muscles during the procedure. I can prescribe something if you like."

"Now, is it safe to take Naprosyn, Ibuprofen, or Tylenol?"

"I prefer you take Tylenol for pain. We will send you home with a couple of Tylenol #3, but take them only if you need them. You may experience a bit of oozing from the surgical sights and that is not unusual, but if any amount more than slight occurs, come to the emergency room."

"O.K. So, what's the course of treatment for what I have going on?"

"You rest. We'll talk more about a treatment regimen on Monday." He got up and left without giving me a chance to ask any more questions.

I closed my eyes and tried to relax. I had been given a lot of information and had already decided I was going to research what I'd been told and talk with the company medical director about appropriate treatment options. I glanced at the clock on the wall; it was 12:15 p.m.

K.C. jumping on my bed startled me awake. I tried to sit up and was quickly reminded by the soreness in my stomach muscles that quick movements weren't such a good idea. Looking around the room, it took me a few minutes to recall all that had taken place and just how I had gotten home. I was still a little fuzzy about the latter.

I looked at my bedside alarm clock; it was 7:19 p.m., and the phone was ringing. It took a little while to maneuver myself into a position so that I could answer the phone.

"Hello?"

"Hi sweetheart! How are you doing? Did I wake you?"

"Well, yeah. I've been sleeping on and off all day."

"You sound groggy. Are you O.K.?"

"Honey, I'm fine. I'm just catching up on a lot of lost sleep from over the past few weeks."

"I thought I'd come down to see you this weekend?"

"I'd really like that. We need to talk anyway."

"About what?"

"I'll tell you when I see you."

"Dan, that's not fair because you know I'm going to wonder what you're talking about."

"Tough! You're going to have to wait until you get here. Besides, I want you to tell me how Christmas was with the kids and family."

"It was all right. It would have been better if you were here."

"Thank you, but we talked about this, and given everything that has happened within your family and mine, we needed to spend time with our families separately."

"I know. I really miss you."

"Joyce, you really have no idea of how many times I wanted to pick up the phone this week and call."

"Why didn't you?"

"Because I didn't want to be a pain."

"Dan, stop it."

"Honey, I don't mean to cut you short, but I have been lying here long enough that I really have to get up and pee."

Laughing, "O.K., honey, I'll let you go. Can I come down on Friday night?"

"You bet. I'm looking forward to it. I'll call you before Friday."

"I think I am in love with you, Mr. Grauer."

"Me too, Mrs. T."

"Bye."

Hanging up the phone, I hoped that the soreness would be gone by Friday. Who was I kidding? I was going to have to tell all. I had promised not to hide anything from Joyce. It was time to fess up. Was it time to tell my family as well? No, not yet. I would wait until after my doctor's visit on Monday.

I decided to try and return to work on Thursday, at least for part of a day. I talked with the company medical director about my condition and diagnosis. He essentially repeated the prognosis and statistics given to me by my doctor. He did tell me that I would most likely need chemotherapy and possibly radiation therapy, depending on how confident the doctor was regarding the tumor removal. The research and information he provided was detailed, but comforting, leaving me with a renewed confidence in my prognosis.

Joyce came down on Friday evening. I was lying on the couch watching TV when she arrived. Her "social worker" knock on the door made me jump and wince at the same time. There was still some tenderness in my stomach muscles that I woudn't be able to hide.

I opened the door and Joyce threw her arms around my neck and planted a kiss on me like it had been years since we had last seen one another. I pulled back just a little, but was enough for her to notice.

"O.K., what's wrong?"

"Nothing, I mean something, I mean, come in and sit down."

It took a few minutes to put together how I wanted to express my thoughts to Joyce. I had indeed promised that I would never lie to her, and while I wanted to spill it all, I was also afraid of driving her away with my problems. My thoughts kept going back to something my dad used to say. "You can only invest so much into a used car before it begins to dollar you to death. When this happens you just need to get rid of it." I was afraid I had begun to hit the throw away threshold.

Looking into Joyce's eyes, the words simply rolled out of my mouth. "Joyce, I have been diagnosed with stomach cancer." Holding up my hand, "Let me finish talking before you say anything."

During the next hour, I poured out my heart, my fears, and my feelings. I filled in the gaps from November to present date with all of the medical information I could remember. Joyce asked questions during my confession, but made no judgments and didn't seem ready to bolt out the door. Instead, she hugged me, kissed me, and said, "We'll make it through this, too!"

Time seemed to stop in the moment that followed. Those minutes are permanently etched into my memory. The gift of unconditional love, kindness, and compassion overwhelmed me. Joyce put her hands on my cheeks and turned my head so that I looked into her eyes. I saw a genuine sincerity and caring that I had not witnessed in a very long time, and, for the first time, while looking into my eyes, she said the words that gave me a true sense of comfort. "Dan Grauer, I love you, and I am in love with you; nothing will change that. I want you to know that I will be here for you when you need me." The commitment was real and now the ball was in my court.

The weekend was awesome. We did nothing and yet talked about everything. Knowing that someone else shared my secret lifted my spirits dramatically. It became painfully obvious that I was going to have to learn how to receive the companionship, tenderness, and love that flowed from Joyce with the same appreciation, thankfulness, and humility that I expected from others when I was the giver. So, what was my hesitation and doubt? I think that somewhere in the back of my brain, for whatever reason, a very small flicker of hope existed, wanting Sara to change, just enough to give me the same unconstrained trust and love that Joyce was willing to commit to, but then, maybe I didn't deserve it.

January 5, was my dad's birthday. Over the past two years, it seemed as though many dates that were normally happy reminders had come and gone, leaving negative impressions. Joyce wanted to stay an extra day and go with me, but I wasn't ready to make our giving reciprocal; not yet anyway.

As I sat in the doctor's office, I glanced at the notes I had made of what I needed to discuss with my doctor from my upcoming sentencing on February 17 and pending incarceration, as well as the medical concerns I had documented. I had waited only a few minutes when I was escorted to an exam room and told the doctor would be with me shortly.

"Dan, how are you feeling?"

"Physically, I am doing all right; mentally, I am a mess."

"We're going to spend about an hour together today. I have some videos I want you to watch and a lot of information to share concerning your treatment plan. I see you took my advice and put together a list of questions to ask."

"I did, along with other information you're going to need to know. Before we get started on the medical front, I need to tell you about what is happening in my personal life as it will effect how we proceed medically."

During the next twenty minutes I explained what I felt the doctor needed to know from January 15, 2001 to the upcoming sentencing date of February 17. As I looked into the doctor's eyes, I saw mixed emotions of surprise as well as sincere concern.

"So, from your sentencing date of February 17 to the date you might have to report to prison will be how long?"

"I don't know. The way my attorney explained it to me is that a report date will be established essentially based on availability. He estimates it could be from March 1 to June 1."

"So, we safely have about eight to twelve weeks to work with. Is that correct?"

"I'd say that's as good as guess as any."

"O.K., let's do this then. I want to start you on chemotherapy right away. We will be using a combination of drugs called ECF. We usually run the chemotherapy treatments in cycles of three-week periods; however, based on what you have told me, we are going to attempt to get four cycles completed in eight weeks' time. This will entail administering the chemotherapy treatments every other week during the next eight weeks. Dan, I have to be honest, this is extremely aggressive, and depending on how you respond to the chemo, we may have to cut back.

"The drugs will be administered intravenously. You will come to the hospital and you can plan on spending at least four hours for each treatment. We will draw blood prior to each treatment to track your white blood cell counts and insure your safety. Side effects of the drugs we will use usually include complete hair loss, fatigue, nausea, diarrhea, and loss of appetite. Not everyone experiences the same side effects."

"How many treatments do you think I might need altogether?"

"That's going to depend on how your body and the cancer respond to the treatments."

"Will I be able to continue working doing the chemotherapy treatments?"

"That, again, will depend on how your body responds to the treatments and reacts to the drug combinations. I think you should be able to."

"Can we do the treatments on Fridays so that I have the weekend to rest?"

"Yes, we can accommodate that."

"How will we know if the treatment is working?"

"We will do another complete scan after the third or fourth cycle and compare the size of the cancerous lesion to its original size. This will also help us determine the length of continued treatment."

About an hour later, I left the office with another page of notes and my head full of information to be processed about my immediate future. I was to report to the hospital on Friday at 8:00 a.m. for my first chemotherapy treatment. I glanced quickly at my notes. I wasn't embellishing the idea of the side effects we discussed, but at least they would advance gradually and not all at once.

I continued to utilize the medical director at work as an informational resource and almost as a second opinion physician. He told me the treatment plan was appropriate and extremely aggressive, but at the same time he encouraged me to focus on becoming healthier as a whole person. I had kept my boss and human resources apprised of the medical developments as well as the legal issues; they were extremely supportive. I was sad knowing that most likely my relationship with a company I had begun to consider "mine" would most likely end in the very near future.

Joyce had wanted to attend the chemotherapy treatments with me, but I just couldn't have her there. I guess I perceived it as a sign of weakness and couldn't give up the last little bit of male pride I had retained. I promised her I would call her on Friday evening, following the initial treatment. She couldn't come down to Omaha this weekend anyway and I found myself almost pouting like a teenager who had lost a best friend.

The first chemotherapy treatment lasted about two and a half hours. I was in a room with others receiving chemotherapy, many of whom the drug's side effects appeared to have taken its toll. I should have brought a book to read and made a mental note to do so in the future. It wasn't the needles, the drugs, or even the coldness with which the room temperature was moderated, but the boredom that created my frustration and impatience. As the drugs were administered, I felt, almost instantaneously, flushed with warmth. I looked around the room to see if anyone noticed my sensation, and as I looked around the room, I wondered how many would survive. How many would be here the next time I came in, or the time after that?

Back in my apartment, I lay on the couch and turned on the television. I was more mentally fatigued than anything. I actually felt pretty good and wondered just how soon the dreaded side effects would begin. I awakened with my heart racing and pounding. I sat up, drenched in sweat, trying to recall the dreams that left me in this state. I remember being in prison and fighting off several attackers, none of whom I could identify as the facial features were merely a blur. The dream was in black and white, except for the crimson color of my blood flowing into the floor drain as I huddled helplessly into a corner.

Returning to the conscious world, I looked at the television, then through the sliding glass door onto my balcony to make sure the dream wasn't real. The vividness with which the events occurred scared me. I had no idea where they came from; maybe the side effects had indeed begun. I got off the couch and slowly walked to the kitchen. K.C. was dancing around my legs as though he needed to go outside so I hooked him to his leash and headed out the door. I wasn't real hungry anyway.

Chapter 26

Focusing on work became a problem; for that matter, focusing on anything became a problem. I couldn't seem to get through any one project or task without distraction and loss of energy. I began missing work simply because I didn't feel like being there I was tired and sad all of the time. Phone conversations with Joyce made only a slight difference in my attitude; I had become short and non-responsive even with her. I seldom talked with my kids and had the social interactions of a hermit. The negativity became so intense that it began to interfere with my ability to work, eat, sleep, and enjoy life. I felt lifeless and empty; activities that I usually enjoyed became an effort in just going through the motions.

I had completed two chemotherapy sessions and began to feel as though I was living in a black hole of some kind. Little things began to frustrate me; being grouchy, irritable, and easily annoyed was the norm. Trapped in my own pessimistic world, I could easily justify exaggerating when it came to any issue. Feeling both hopeless and helpless, I began to think dying was the best alternative.

On January 30, 2004, I acted on that irrationality for the second time in six months. Having been a paramedic in the military, I knew that an overdose of insulin would cause diabetic coma due to extreme low blood sugars, eventually leading to death. I also knew that the insulin would quickly dissolve into the blood stream and suicide would be extremely difficult to prove, allowing for the collection of life insurance money, which, in turn, could be used to end the financial burdens I had brought upon my family.

Despite the irrationality of these thoughts, the rational side of me knew that this was merely an attempt to get some attention by whatever means necessary. My brain was waging an all-out battle between living and dying. Dying could solve our financial woes, but leave my family devastated. Living would still leave my family emotionally devastated and in a financial black hole. If I attempted suicide and failed, it would be deemed as merely another failure attributed to not doing it right the first time and, in my own mind, be typical of my life to date.

I only remember the police coming through my door followed by the paramedics. I was transported to the hospital via ambulance. I remember seeing Sara and my daughter, Tiffany, and wondered how they had gotten into my apartment. I wouldn't become conscious of my surroundings until I awoke in the psyche ward, again. Another failure, what was next?

I was hooked up to a heart and respiratory monitor and an IV bag hung next to the bed. The nurse roused me into a semiconscious state, insisting on taking my blood pressure despite my need to sleep. Breakfast was brought into the room and I was told I had to eat. The staff was no non-sense about what was expected of me and the treatment plan that would be implemented.

Saturday afternoon would be comprised of a complete psychological exam and battery of testing. I would be ordered to follow up with the staff psychiatrist at the clinic next to the hospital with prearranged appointments. I was going to spend at least one more day in the hospital despite my wishes and I would only be released into the care of someone willing to take responsibility for me. I wanted to call Joyce and talk with her, but I was embarrassed about having hit the bottom of the barrel for a second time. I couldn't do that to her.

Sara and Alisha came to visit in the afternoon. Tiffany and Alisha were extremely upset and angry, and rightfully so. Sara appeared unemotional and unresponsive to all that had taken place. The conversation was tense and awkward.

I tried to justify to both of them the reasoning behind my actions, but couldn't find the right words. It's difficult to explain to someone what feelings pushed me to cross the threshold of selfishness into a world of self-pity, sorrow, and sadness where suicide seemed to be the best option.

Sunday afternoon came and the doctor felt as though I could be released with outpatient follow-up. The one stipulation was that I was to be released into the supervision of another adult. Did I call Joyce and tell her, or did I ask Sara? I was way beyond embarrassed and there was no way I could call Joyce, so I elected to ask Sara. Sara, Alisha, and Tiffany came to see me about 4:00 p.m. I could tell by looking in her eyes that Sara didn't want me to be released under her supervision. I am certain had it not been for the kids, she would not have agreed to it. I merely wanted her to take me back to my apartment; however, Sara's idea of supervision was quite literal and she insisted that if she agreed to this, I would stay at least one night on her couch. I reluctantly agreed, thinking that once released I could talk her into taking me back to my place.

Little did I know that this day would become etched not only into my memory and generate a fear within my kids I had never before seen. Sara insisted that I stay on the couch at their apartment; she had signed her name as being responsible for me and as such she would not even consider letting me stay on my own. I felt like a child being punished, having to stand with my nose in the corner. I was not in a good mood.

Upon entering the apartment, the first thing I noticed was a big bouquet of flowers on the table. Being the male chauvinist pig that I am, I walked directly to them and read the card. They were from some guy Sara was seeing. I retreated to the couch and tried to rest; the girls went to their rooms to finish homework and sort laundry. Sara went to the bedroom. I heard Sara's cell phone ring and when she answered it the door to the bedroom went shut. The apartment walls were thin and it didn't take very much to know that she was most likely talking with the same guy who had sent her the flowers.

As I stretched out on the couch, it dawned on me that our lives had truly grown apart. I briefly reflected on our twenty years of marriage. What had happened? I'm not sure whether I was struck with panic or anxiety, but I became overwhelmed with the feeling that I needed to leave! I didn't belong there anymore! As I got up to walk out, Alisha came out and asked me what was going on.

"I just need to leave. I'm no longer a part of what goes on here. I am extremely uncomfortable in this situation and just need to be by myself."

"Dad, you can't leave. I'm going to tell mom. "MOM! MOM! DAD'S TRYING TO LEAVE!"

Sara came out of the bedroom closing her cell phone as she walked. "Dan, you can't leave. I took responsibility for you and I take that seriously."

"Sara, I don't belong here anymore. I'm not going to get any rest with things like those flowers on the table."

"What's the matter, can't handle it, knowing that I am dating someone?"

"No, that's not it at all. How would you feel inside my apartment if a big bouquet of flowers sat on the table from Joyce? Would you feel comfortable?"

"How does it feel? How do you like it knowing that I don't need you?"

"Sara, stop it. I'm leaving."

Sara stepped into the dining area and picked up the phone. "Go ahead. I'll call the police and you'll be right back in the hospital."

"Sara, that's not even funny. I'm fine. I just need to be by myself," I said, walking toward the door.

Sara began to dial. I'm truly not sure what happened next, but I believe that all the medications, emotions, and recent events came together and incited a rage never before seen inside of me. I grabbed the phone and broke it into two pieces, walked over, and pulled the cord out of the wall breaking it as well. As I walked toward the door to leave, Sara stepped in front of me. I grabbed her arm and meant to throw her on the loveseat sitting a few feet away. What happened and what I saw scared even me! Sara went over the back of the loveseat in the air and landed hard on the floor. Alisha and Tiffany and both screamed at me to stop. I walked to the door and left.

I next remember the cold and wet feeling physically taking hold of my body. I was approximately three blocks away from Sara's apartment, no coat or hat, looking up at the stoplight as it changed from green to yellow and then red. I turned back toward the direction from which I came and saw Sara walking after me about a block away. What the hell had I done? Never before had I laid a hand on Sara, and was brought up knowing that it was wrong. I was actually more ashamed of what had just taken place than of the stupidity that led to my dismissal from the railroad.

As I watched Sara get closer, I couldn't hear what she was saying, but her face told the whole story. She was scared and hesitant to come near me. I crumpled and let Sara lead me back to the apartment.

Once again on the couch, I turned so that I faced the back and mentally departed into a totally different world. Sleep was not to be found on this night. I had, once again, crossed the line going beyond what I knew to be right. Reality had become so painful, depressing, and unmanageable that I felt as though I was becoming a monster. I left Sara's apartment early the next morning using the excuse that I needed to get to my place, shower, change clothes, and head back into work.

I didn't go to work, but instead retreated to my bedroom in a futile attempt to get some rest. I looked at the clock and it was about 11:00 a.m. I couldn't take lying around anymore. I was embarrassed and ashamed of what had taken place throughout the entire weekend and needed to apologize to both Sara and the girls. I got dressed and headed out the door, grabbing the antacid as I walked by the dining room table.

I knew that Sara would come home for lunch. As I drove toward her apartment and drank the chalky, thick, nasty-tasting liquid, I tried to compose the words that needed to be said. Over and over again in my mind I attempted to find just the right words, but I was having difficulty because nothing I could say would justify my actions.

Before I was ready, I found myself pulling into Sara's apartment complex. I walked upstairs and knocked on the door.

"Why are you even here? I don't want to talk to you."

"Sara, we need to talk. I need to tell you how sorry I am."

Opening the door, she walked past me and started down the stairs. "I'm late for work and I need to get back. There's nothing else to say."

"Sara, give me five minutes."

"No, I've don't want to have anything to do with you."

Following her out the main entrance, "Sara, then let me talk with the girls and apologize to them."

"You stay away from them; I am seriously considering getting a restraining order against you."

By this time we were at her car. She had opened the door and had gotten inside to start the car. I grabbed her arm just above the elbow to get her attention and Sara did something I totally did not anticipate. She screamed at the top of her lungs as though I were going to kill her. The more I asked her to stop, the more she screamed. I was horrified. I didn't know what to do, so I reached out and slapped her across the face. I'm not sure who was more shocked, Sara, or I She did stop screaming and looked at me with eyes that were overflowing with venom. "I hate you! I don't ever want to see you again."

As I watched her drive away, I remember thinking, "Well, that went really well, didn't it, Dan, you dumb ass." I got back in my car and drove home wondering just how bad things could get.

The days seemed extensively long and the nights even longer. I had begun to wake up every morning with my bed full of hair as though I had begun shedding much like K.C. does. It wasn't too bad until patches of hair began to fall off; that's when I decided to go ahead and give myself a new look. I shaved my head. I figured at this point what I looked like was the least of my worries.

February 17, my sentencing day, came quickly. I had spent the last couple of weeks trying to get my "shit" together. I worked hard trying to not leave any projects undone for my employer, not knowing what was going to happen. Joyce wanted to come down for the hearing, but I didn't get a sense that she was ready to walk into a Federal Courthouse again, so I told her, "No." My brothers all came to Omaha.

Dave, my oldest brother, stayed the night with me. I couldn't bring myself to thank him for all that he had done for me for fear of unleashing more tears. As we were getting ready to leave, Dave recommended I read a couple of Bible passages that may help with the anxiety. I doubted that much of anything was going to help at this point. I sat down at the dining room table and began to read. I have to admit, that as I read each word, a feeling of calmness and comfort began to overtake my heart. Finally, I was ready, or at least as ready as I could get.

I met with Allen briefly before the hearing and was told Judge Michaels would review the charges and make sure that I understood what they were and what was taking place today. He said that after all was said and done, I would have an opportunity just prior to sentencing to speak if I chose to do so. I already knew that I needed to tell those with me just how sorry I was and accept responsibility for my actions. I knew I would never find the right words to express my guilt, sorrow, and shame, but I needed to try.

Allen and my brother, Dave, were off talking about something. I later discovered that Dave had paid my legal fees in full. Pastor Craig was present and provided some words of support to both my family and I. My brothers, Doug and Dennis, had also come to Omaha to support me. As I waited outside the assigned courtroom, I saw Sara and one of her best friends walk into the courtroom.

Finally, Allen said it was time. I walked into the courtroom with my head held high and an eerie calmness in my heart. My family followed us in, as did Pastor Craig. Sara and her friend were sitting off to the left. Four or five other persons were already seated in the courtroom; I suspected they were representatives of the insurance company that had reimbursed the railroad for my indiscretion and possibly a representative from the railroad itself.

I sat to Allen's right at a table also located on the right front side of the courtroom as we faced the bench. To our left was the Federal prosecutor. The hearing began with the bailiff announcing the entry of the Honorable Judge Lyle Michaels. Judge Michaels took control of the hearing, listening first to the Federal prosecutor, then to Allen. When he was convinced he had heard all he needed, Judge Michaels asked me to stand. He asked several questions to insure I indeed understood what was taking place and that I felt Allen had done an adequate job of representing me. He asked if I wanted to address the court.

An outpouring of emotion came forth. I'm not sure what words were said, but I tried to apologize to the railroad and my family. I took full responsibility for my actions, although, I had no answer for "why." When I could think of no more, I sat down.

Judge Michaels politely asked me to stand again. He told me of the numerous letters he had received from my family and friends telling him of the suffering I had gone through as a result of my mistake. The letters from my children told of the type of father I had been and my brothers had written letters of support detailing my remorse. He had read each and every one of them very carefully. I later learned that each of my children, my mom, my brothers, and Joyce had written to Judge Michaels; the one disappointment was that Sara had not, twenty years of marriage meant nothing.

Finally, Judge Michaels looked at me and said, "Mr. Grauer, while I truly believe you are remorseful and sorry for what you have done, I cannot let this incident go unpunished. I hereby sentence you to twelve months and one day of incarceration at the Federal correctional facility in Yankton, South Dakota." He then went on to explain that if he had sentenced me to anything less, I would not be eligible for "good behavior time." In this way I would serve approximately ten months incarceration. I sat back down and began to sort through what I had just heard.

The last item of discussion was when the sentence would begin. Allen asked that I be allowed to see my daughter, Tiffany, graduate high school at the end of May. Judge Michaels denied this request and my report date was set for April 5, 2004. The hearing was adjourned.

As we walked from the courtroom, Allen explained that I was free to continue living as I had been, but that I must report no later than 2:00 p.m. on April 5, 2004, to the correctional facility in Yankton. He said the probation office would be providing me with written documentation on what needed to be done. As we left the courtroom, my brothers gathered around us. Allen stated that I would need to go to the U.S. Marshal's office for processing before I left and that $200 must be paid to the Clerk of the District Court today. I told Allen, I didn't have that much in my account. My brother, Doug, stepped forward and said he would take care of it.

Dave, Doug, Dennis, Allen, and Pastor Craig began a discussion as I started downstairs toward the U.S. Marshal's office. Dave stopped long enough to instruct me to come back upstairs and find them so that we could go to lunch. I told him that I didn't know if I could eat anything, but that I wanted to spend time with them.

Inside the U.S. Marshal's office, I was fingerprinted, photographed, and assigned a Federal prison number. They gave me a very detailed and lengthy set of instructions, including how often I needed to report to the U.S. Probation Office and some limited information about the Federal prison in Yankton, South Dakota.

As I walked up the two flights of stairs to join my brothers, my mind was a whirlwind of thoughts both good and bad. Waiting three years to be prosecuted was going to be followed with another three months' wait to pay the price for my indiscretions; I hoped and prayed that both mentally and physically I could hang on. I began to plan in my mind all that needed to be done prior to reporting to prison on April 5.

There is a good Mexican restaurant, Michaels, in the Old Market area; we decided to walk there for lunch. The walk was full of encouraging words from my brothers and continued commitments of support. Doug said that I needed to call mom; I told him that I wasn't sure I could, but I also knew in my heart this was necessary. My oldest brother, Dave, said that he had invited Sara to come along to lunch so that she would know their intentions on making sure that she and the kids were taken care of; she refused, and I think he was truly disappointed by her.

I wasn't real hungry, but enjoyed the time with my brothers. We talked about my prison expectations and how they could help. I told them that child support would be the biggest issue; I didn't know how I could come up with the $800 plus per month during my incarceration. Dave told me not to worry about it. I told them I was planning on signing the title of the car over to Sara; she could do with it what she wanted. If she wanted to use it for a trade in, or sell it, that would be fine. Finally, the time came for them to leave and I was alone once again. Sleep didn't appear to be an option, at least not on this day.

At about 5:00 a.m., I got into the shower and stayed until the hot water ran out. As I stood under the hot water, letting it rush down the back of my neck and back, I wished that I could wash away my past and watch it disappear down the drain; however, I knew this wasn't reality. At about 6:30 a.m. I headed into work. I needed to tell both my supervisor and the Director of human resources the outcome of the sentencing proceedings.

I met first with my supervisor. Cameron was a mild-mannered man, with an extensive knowledge and years of experience in the insurance industry. He was supportive of most any project that would make the company better regarding the work processes, and very supportive of any personal undertaking that would make us better individuals. Cameron listened intently as I explained all that had taken place at the hearing. I had hidden nothing from them; however, this was not the outcome they had hoped for. When I was finished, Cameron sat in silence for what seemed like an eternity and then said, "Dan, I don't know what to say. We have been extremely fortunate to have you with us and have appreciated all you have done. I am going to have to take this information up a level and see what decision, if any, needs to be made. Have you told human resources yet?"

"No, they are my next stop."

"Meet with them and then come and see me."

As I walked out of Cameron's office toward the elevator, my stomach began to ache and feel as though burning coals were inside it. I knew what was coming and I guess I really couldn't blame them. Following my discussions with the Director of human resources, I walked slowly back to my office mulling over the future.

I sat down at my desk and began to log into the computer when Cameron appeared from around the corner. He said, "Dan, the decision that has been made was not my choice, but, as of this moment, you have a choice of resigning or of being terminated. However, because of all you have done for us we are going to pay you through April 5, 2004. My recommendation is that you take a few minutes and compose a resignation letter. Bring it to me for approval and make sure to include the pay arrangements. I am going to leave a box for your personal belongings and will escort you from the building once the resignation is signed. I'm truly sorry. . ."

"Cameron, it's O.K. I understand and I truly appreciate the opportunity you have given me and the fact that you think enough of my work to pay me through April 5." We shook hands and I turned to author my resignation.

Returning to the apartment, I was focused on two thoughts: First, it actually would be kind of nice to be off and truly get prepared for April 5, and second I didn't want to be off because that was going to give me way too much time to think of the worst possible scenarios. I needed to make plans for storage of my furniture, pay any outstanding bills, and make sure the kids knew I was going to be O.K. It was the last of these that would be the struggle.

I called Joyce and talked with her for a long time. There were so many things I wanted to tell her. She had become my best friend and guardian angel. Joyce had the ability to reach me on so many levels that others could not. Joyce and I had built a foundation of honesty, openness, and new levels of expression, that to this day is the stronghold in our relationship. She had become someone with whom I could share triumphs and tragedies, joys, and sorrows. A person with whom I could enjoy a sunset or a football game, a friend with whom I could talk, or not talk and either was O.K. She opened up a world of emotions that I didn't know could exist in a relationship, but I was also determined that my life was in the hands of God, not Dan's. I had already tried twice and failed, so either I wasn't serious or God wanted me around yet for something unknown to me.

I focused the next weeks on my health, and preparing both physically and mentally for entering the world of incarceration. Despite discussions with Allen, my fears sometimes got the best of me and I would wake up in a "cold sweat."

I made a point to stay away from Sara, and talked with the kids on the phone. Alisha stayed with me occasionally, but not as often as I would have liked. I enjoyed taking walks with K.C. and became more comfortable giving my life back to God, hoping, praying, and trusting my future would be good.

I don't remember what day it was, but out of the blue, Sara called.

"Dan, I would like to drive you up to Yankton. I think it's going to be important that the kids have a chance to spend some time with you."

"Well, Sara, I too believe it's important for the kids to come along, but I want someone who will hug me, look me in the eye, tell me they love me, and mean it."

The phone line went silent; I knew she was contemplating what I had said.

"So, does that mean you want Joyce to take you to Yankton?"

"That's not what I said. I said, whoever it is needs to be able to do those things. I need to know that whoever drops me off will stand by me, and be there for me when I get out. I know the kids love me and they will be there for me."

Again, the phone line went silent, with neither of us saying anything.

"I'll call you back. I have to go to work," and Sara hung up.

I stood for what seemed like a long time with the phone to my ear, wondering if Sara could or even wanted to do what I had asked. I walked to the couch and lay down. Did I want Sara back? If Sara was able to say the words I wanted to hear, would that be enough to save our marriage? I didn't think so, but I didn't dismiss that possibility either.

March 19 was my last treatment. I was feeling good both physically and mentally, but was becoming more and more anxious about April 5. Sara was insisting on driving me to Yankton. I had the feeling that would be the only way I would be able to see the kids. I had tried to hammer home the idea that I really needed to know that Sara could say the words I longed to hear, but she continued to be elusive. I had tried to get all of my affairs in order. I had given Sara my checkbook and left money in the account, and signed my car title over to her. I had talked with my older brother, Dave, who assured me I needn't worry about the child support. What little furniture I kept, I had put into storage.

Yankton, South Dakota was about three hours from Council Bluffs. I had to report to the prison no later than 2:00 p.m. We left around 9:00 a.m. Sara, Tiffany, Alisha, and I began a journey that certainly became a pivotal point in my life and my future.

We arrived in Yankton around 12:15 p.m. The kids were hungry, so we found a Dairy Queen. My nerves were on edge and I had no appetite. After lunch we drove by the prison facility. The facility looked really laid-back from the outside; it was an old college campus and was well maintained. I remember thinking, "Maybe this wouldn't be so bad. I could do it."

Sara asked, "Do you want to find a park and just kill some time?"

"NO! The sooner I get there, the sooner I get out."

We parked on the west side of the facility and walked to the building we were directed to by the signs posted. The tears began to swell and a lump the size of an apple formed in my throat. The girls began to cry and hugged me, not wanting to let go. All I could do was apologize for my stupidity. A guard stepped outside and said, "Come on, it's time."

Tears were streaming from my eyes uncontrollably. Sara stepped in front of me; I said, "Remember what I said?" Tears were in her eyes. She gave me a half-hearted hug, turned, and walked away without saying another word. I guess I had my answer. The girls were still crying as we waved to one another. I entered the door of the prison facility and began the processing.

Chapter 27

The first hour consisted of reviewing all the rules and expectations of living inside the Federal prison. A drug test was completed and I was ushered to another building to get my official entry attire. My first strip search occurred within an hour of arriving at the facility. Little did I know that getting naked, bending over spreading my butt cheeks, lifting my testicles, lifting my tongue, and showing the backs of my ears would become routine. I was issued an orange jump suit, blue slip-on boat shoes, sheets, a blanket, a pillow, and given instructions on how to proceed.

Two other men were being processed at the same time. We were escorted across the length of the facility to the housing unit where we were assigned. It was obvious we were "fresh meat," because all other prisoners wore khaki pants, shirts, and boots or tennis shoes; the standard attire appeared to be outdated military uniforms. Not a word was spoken during the trek. The buildings, former college dorms, were actually well-kept and clean. Later, I learned that we would be assigned jobs that paid anywhere from $.15 to $.25 per hour and that many of these jobs surrounded the cleaning of the facility and upkeep of the prison grounds.

We were assigned a counselor who would meet with us at some point during the next week to tell us what classes we would be expected to take during our incarceration, review our sentence length, and insure we understood the rules, expectations, and requirements to be released.

The three of us were then escorted to a basement room and assigned bunks. Our room was approximately 16' by 16', painted light green with outdated floor tile, iron bunk beds, metal lockers, and bars over the windows; it was to be considered "home." This particular room housed eight men of varying races, cultures and had committed various crimes. Each room housed from six to fourteen. There was one restroom per floor with multiple urinals, toilets, and showers.

The break room was also in the basement; in the evenings this would be the center of socialization. The building had one TV room that held approximately forty chairs and two televisions also located in the basement. The laundry facility for the building was on the far side of the break room and consisted of approximately eight washers and dryers; these seemed to be in use during a majority of the free time allotted to each prisoner, throughout the week.

I was assigned the top bunk, along the far wall of our room. Of the eight men assigned to the room, five were lying around reading. At 4:00 p.m., I heard a guard bellow, "Stand for count!" One of the inmates began to explain that at 4:00 p.m. we were expected to stand by our bunks and be counted to insure everyone was present. Absolutely no talking was allowed. Body counts happened at 4:00 p.m., 10:00 p.m., 4:00 a.m., and 10:00 a.m. During any one of these counts, if someone was not where they were to be, the entire facility was locked down until that person was accounted for. The 4:00 a.m. count was the one I never got used to. It was against the rules for an inmate to cover up his head while sleeping, and during this count, the guard, who seemed to have a larger than usual set of keys jingling from his belt, would come strolling into the room, shine a flashlight in our eyes, and count out the number of inmates in each room. Even following my release from prison, it took many, many months not to wake up at the expected times.

At 4:30 p.m., mail call began. I learned that mail was handed out alphabetically, once a day, so that all of the inmates were not packed into one room at the same time. Generally, it was divided up into those inmates whose last name began with A – G, H – O, and P - Z. We were to proceed upstairs to the main entryway and stand quietly while a guard read the names on the incoming mail. Again, any talking might result in the mail being held until a later time; numerous control measures were in place to let the inmates know who was in charge. All incoming mail was opened and read by the prison administration prior to being handed out. I was given a list surrounding the rules of mail both going out and coming into the facility.

When all of the mail had been handed out, it was time for dinner. The "chow" hall was on the other end of the facility and there was also a limited number of inmates it could hold at one time. The order for attending dinner was called by building and alternating as to which housing facility went to dinner first.

The food was prepared and served by inmates assigned to work in the kitchen. Some of them were actually in the process of earning a two-year culinary degree. The menus were changed daily, but became extremely predictable as to what would be served during the week. When the announcement for dinner came, it was like a cattle stampede heading out to pasture. Dinner call was one of the few chances to socialize with those that were considered trustworthy, although I learned there were rules for dinner as well. A time limit was given for eating and returning to the building. The food was good, but I quickly learned that it was necessary to watch what I ate for fear of the worst kind of constipation.

It was quickly becoming apparent that all of the freedoms that I had taken for granted outside of the prison facility could not be taken for granted inside. Following dinner, it was mandatory that everyone return to their housing facility where we were given time for some limited freedoms, such as: going to the break or TV room, doing laundry, going to the gym to workout or play racquetball, softball, or basketball, going to the prison library, going to the church if a service or function was being held, or if the weather was nice, just sitting outside on the park-type of benches. Since this was my first night of incarceration, I chose to simply lie in my bunk and read the entire "do's and don'ts" of prison life.

When it was time for lights-out, I lay wide awake, staring at the ceiling, wondering what the future held. A peaceful night's sleep was another freedom I had taken for granted that wasn't to be had, at least not on this night.

Tuesday morning began with the 4:00 a.m. body count; I was initiated to the sound of jingling keys and a flashlight beam in my face. Following this count, many of the inmates began heading for the showers and their job assignments if they worked the kitchen duty on the breakfast shift. Others stayed in bed electing not to eat, but cherish a few more minutes of sleep before reporting to their assigned jobs at 8:00 a.m.. I tried to watch and learn the routine as quickly as possible in order to blend into the population unnoticed.

Much like the military, beds were to be made each day in a set fashion. At 7:45 a.m. the facility emptied out, except for those assigned to clean the rooms within the building. I was not going to be an exception; I was directed to the mops and buckets, and given explicit orders on exactly what to clean and how to clean it. The meeting with my counselor was scheduled for 10:00 a.m., so for two hours I was expected to keep busy.

I was glad when the loudspeaker page came for me to report to the counselor's office. Upon knocking at the door, I was summoned in and told to sit in the chair across from the desk. My counselor was a middle-aged woman, who had obviously done this type of initiation hundreds of times; there was no variation in the tone of her voice and it was as though she expected to be treated with disregard. A presorted packet was handed to me and I was told to review each page carefully.

Telephone and visitation privileges were explained; each had an associated paper to be completed and returned. Anyone on the approved calling list and visitation list had to be pre-approved by the Bureau of Prisons. I would not have phone privileges in place for three or four days and visitation wouldn't happen for the first fifteen to twenty days. Telephone calls were based on a set number of minutes each prisoner was allowed based on money that was put into a calling card account. It began to dawn on me that for this first week I was on my own. My ability to make decisions with regard to my family was extremely limited, and would be implemented only if my family chose to do so; after all, what was I going to do about it if they didn't?

We reviewed potential job openings within the facility. It was suggested that I visit with the Director of Education. Within the prison system, it was mandatory for those men who did not graduate high school to attend GED classes. A GED certificate was issued to those that successfully completed the program. The "white-collar" criminals who had some educational background were generally recruited to assist in teaching the GED classes. It was made very clear that if I didn't get the "O.K." to work in the education department, I would be scrubbing floors or peeling potatoes.

Finally, I was directed to report to the clothing issue facility and pick up the mandatory uniform that included work boots, underwear, socks, t-shirts, and retired khaki uniforms sets. If I wanted tennis shoes to work out in, I needed to buy them at the commissary where prisoners were allowed to shop, via filling out a checklist once a week. Toiletries such as soap, toothpaste, toothbrush, comb, and laundry soap were issued there as well on one set day of the month.

Directions were given regarding exactly how I could leave the facility and when. Each prisoner must sign in and out upon leaving and entering any building. If I were caught outside without permission, the appropriate punishment would be implemented. With that I was dismissed with one final comment. "Mr. Grauer, read and study all the information I have given you, attend all the required classes, follow the rules, and you will survive your prison sentence."

By the time the 4:00 p.m. count arrived, I had reviewed all of the paperwork given to me, picked up the required clothing and accessories, and had begun to develop a sense for the daily routine. For the first time since my arrival thirty some hours ago, I was hungry and felt like I could join the herd for dinner call.

Returning to the housing facility, I spent some time talking with one of the men assigned to my room regarding additional questions I had about prison life. I found that limited groceries could be purchased, as well as radios with headsets, sweatpants, tennis shoes, and various fitness gear. I listened carefully as he described the process of having money put into a prison account, attending various church functions, the prison library, and the prison recreational facility. Other men in the room would add information and suggestions to make prison life an acceptable routine. Much like a sponge, I absorbed every word.

As I listened, I quickly discovered that along with all of the written rules, there was an unspoken prison code of conduct only presented in a generally unacceptable fashion: do not cry, show fear, or vulnerability publicly. Doing so would quickly make you a target for other prisoners. Learn to play spades, pinochle, pitch or pool. Get a prison job which would keep you occupied and help the days pass more quickly. Read a lot. They have a library here, so use it; catch up on reading you hadn't had time to do. Consider writing as well; letters to friends and family could make time pass a bit faster. Work out; it will make the time go by faster, and is an outlet for stress. In addition, physically fit people are less likely to be targeted as victims for strong-arm tactics.

Brace yourself for the social dynamics of prison. There were specific ways to behave towards others if you wanted to get by: (1) If confronted to become another inmate's sexual toy, fight and continue to fight. You will gain at least some measure of respect for fighting back. NEVER GIVE IN; (2) Do not snitch. If you see something illegal or violent, walk away and do not divulge any information if questioned later. Being known as a snitch would make bad things happen to you; (3) Stick up for yourself. It's better to get into a fight and lose, than to be seen cowering or placating. Your reputation is more important than your desire to avoid pain, so guard it with your life. Ultimately, you should avoid any confrontation if you can, but if you can't avoid one, react quickly and with aggression.

Beware of rape.

Keep to yourself, keep your mouth shut, and do not tell anyone about your personal life, family, or criminal history; trust might lead to betrayal. Do not lie and say you are in for something more serious than the crime you for which you were convicted; you could get into a lot of trouble with other inmates for lying.

Don't get involved in other inmates' business.

Recognize that nights are the worst. You will miss your family, and freedom. You will probably cry, but you had better stifle it into your pillow so no one will hear. Stay in contact with friends and family. Letters, cards, and the occasional phone call will really help you maintain your sanity and an active role with your family. You may be out of sight for a while, but there is no reason to stay out of mind.

Respect the prison staff. While they are not there to help you, disrespecting them could make your time here worse, but don't get too friendly; they will turn on you too as there is an economic system in prison, and it involves staff, too. They have reasons to use you as well.

If your time is getting short, or if you are being transferred to a lesser facility, DON'T tell anyone. Out of spite, some convicts will get a sick glee from getting you sent to the "hole" or lengthening your time. Make careful choices regarding your "friends" and your location at any given moment of the day. Avoid drug use and tattoos; both are prominent inside the prison walls.

Just like in the real world, in prison there are gangs, but in prison, gangs are far more prevalent. These gangs, despite what people would like to believe, are an integral part of the functionality of the prison system. However, they work very differently on the inside than on the outside. Be mindful of gang members, but avoid joining a gang. Gang members are soldiers, and gang leaders demand absolute loyalty. If you join a gang, you may be ordered to do something that would keep you in prison much longer

Finally, above all, remember that the normal rules of the outside world simply no longer apply. When you're in prison, you're living on a different planet where all that matters is surviving the experience with as little damage as possible.

My head was spinning; was all of this merely a bunch of hype? I felt that some of the advice, while well intentioned, was meant to scare the "newbie" inmate. I was confident that I would be fine.

I had been so physically and spiritually out of shape, that my main goal was to spend the next ten plus months strengthening both attributes. I was determined and committed to become the man I knew I needed to be for myself and my family. My real job was simple: get myself right with God, my children, my family, and become more physically fit.

At about 9:00 p.m., I decided to take a shower. Having observed this task as accomplished by others, I knew that I would walk in flip-flops, wrapped in a towel, and carrying my clean clothing and toiletries to the bathroom facility. If someone else was in the shower, the long handled shower squeegee would be blocking the entryway into the shower. In this way, some privacy could be had since this was the smallest of bathroom facilities in the building. The squeegee was against the wall and not placed kitty-corner in the doorway, so the shower was free.

The hot water felt good and I began to relax. I had lathered my head with soap and began to rinse when I heard a low, growling, calculating voice announce, "FRESH MEAT! You're about to be welcomed to prison!" I turned to see three men, naked, all facing me. One of them had begun masturbating, saying, "Come to papa, boy!" I guess the wisdom of other prisoners was about to become reality.

I honestly don't recall, or maybe my mind refuses to recall, what happened next. What I do know, is that my next point of reality was when the hot water turned cold, like a scene from some horrible movie; I was cowering in the corner of the shower, curled up into a fetal position. I couldn't breathe, my heart was pounding, trying to escape my chest, and every muscle in my body twitched with an almost seizure type of contraction. I could move my arms and my legs, but I had apparently become so tense that my muscles ached as I began to move, so I stood up and took a small step almost falling flat once again. I didn't think any bones were broken, but I was bleeding, and where I was bleeding from scared the hell out of me. No one had to tell me what had taken place, I knew.......

I sat down on the wooden bench just inside the shower stall and tried to focus. "O.K., Dan, you're in prison. So who do you report this to? Or, do you even report it? If I report it, what are the consequences? The spoken words of a conversation just fifteen minutes prior with my other roommates rang loudly in my head. Would I even be believed? This was supposed to be a minimum security prison. How was this allowed to happen?"

"Hey, man, you about done?"

"Yeah, give me a minute," I tried to say without showing the pain or fear in my voice. I did my best to rinse the blood out of my washcloth and towel hoping that the bleeding had stopped so that it wouldn't soak through the clean underwear I had put on. I left the bathroom and walked slowly toward my bunk, another sleepless night. Just how much more could I take? How much more could God take away from me?

Chapter 28

As I lay awake contemplating what to do next, an eerie calmness swept my body and mind. With every fiber of my being, I was given a sense of confidence that the worst was now over, that I could begin to heal, if only I would listen to His guidance and direction and unconditionally give up total control of my life to Him. Humility and humbleness had both taken center stage in my current life style. Could I let go of the anger? How could I forgive? I had only my physical life left to lose; my pride, my ego, any sense of masculinity, and all of my material possessions had been taken, and at this particular moment in time, I really didn't care if that was taken from me as well.

Following the 4:00 a.m. head count, I got up, grabbed my Bible, and walked to the break room. I had never read much from the Bible, and I really didn't know where or how to start, but I also knew that finding spiritual guidance was going to be a huge step; in reality, it was the only alternative left in prison survival. I decided to start at the beginning of both the Old Testament and New Testament, and read for a minimum of sixty minutes. My Bible, a men's devotional bible, was given to me by my brother, Dave, as a Christmas present. I sat down, opened to Matthew, and began reading. Mentally, I had developed a plan to read thirty minutes in the New Testament and thirty minutes of the Old Testament. Additionally, every few pages contained Christian testimony and witness from famous athletes, writers, politicians, actors, and other influential people. I had calculated the days I had remaining in prison and knew that if I could come close to this accomplishment, I could read the entire Bible through twice during my stay.

I know that at that very moment, God opened the doors of my heart to hear His word. In what seemed seconds, but in reality was well over an hour, I was given a new direction, energy, and focus to learn the true meaning of life. In just over an hour, excitement and enthusiasm overcame all other emotions; I began to look forward to the lessons, teaching, and knowledge that would be imparted upon me over the next months. I began by asking for forgiveness, direction, and guidance; this quickly led to discovering that life is not about materialism, nor what others think of you, and it's not about what you take from life, but what you leave behind.

I had been granted permission to work in the education department, assisting inmates in obtaining their GEDs. We had to be in our work areas by 8:00 a.m., and were done by 4:00 p.m. Generally, there was an hour given for lunch, but only a limited amount of that time could actually be spent in the dining hall. Any "rehabilitation" class that was assigned was mandatory attendance. I soon learned that these classes appeared to be directed at teaching me how much of a "low life" I really was, and how much pain I had inflicted upon my countless victims.

In reality, they didn't teach me anything with which I hadn't already punished myself. There was nothing that I could make up for the humility, anguish, and pain I had caused in so many lives due to shear stupidity on my part. What I did learn was that my outlook regarding my mistakes was vastly different than those held by a majority of the inmates. I was willing to take responsibility and accountability for my indiscretions.

The job itself equated to being a teacher's assistant, and for those inmates who were truly dedicated to making a positive change in their lives, this became one of my greatest personal rewards. GED testing was given periodically, and to see the heartfelt emotions that passing the GED brought to some inmates was awesome, many of whom did their best to say "Thanks" for the tutelage. Some college courses were available, and it was always gratifying to see those that had been in a GED class move on to higher education. Most, however, knew that they would return to the same habits of their previous life: making thousands of dollars per week as a drug dealer was more appealing than working at a $10 per hour job.

The evenings were filled with listening to stories of street life, stories of "what not to do next time so I don't get caught," and "had it not been for so-and-so I wouldn't be here." I would guess that less than 20 percent of the inmates took full responsibility for their actions or crimes. It was a time to read, write letters, reflect on the past, and plan the future. A lack of sleep had begun to take a physical toll on my body, as weariness and weakness took hold.

Finally, Friday night came. April 9, 2004 became another date etched into my mind. It was on this date I learned another very valuable lesson about prison. I had finally received phone privileges to call my immediate family, or those that had submitted the proper paperwork, which included Joyce. I missed her terribly, and needed just to hear her voice; I had so many questions that I just knew she could help with. As I dialed the phone my hands began to tremble with anticipation of hearing someone familiar on the other end of the phone. It was during this conversation I learned that ALL phone calls are recorded and monitored. I told Joyce about my "shower incident," although, being a man and letting my pride get in the way, it was an embellished version. I told Joyce everything, but improvised a story about fighting back. I guess I was ashamed and embarrassed to admit that I apparently had done nothing except pass out; I really didn't remember.

Less than thirty minutes after hanging up the receiver, I was paged to the office of the Captain of prison guards. He replayed my phone conversation, and demanded to know exactly what happened.

I admitted to lying to Joyce and told him the unembellished version of my prison welcoming. He listened and asked questions as I talked. He was frustrated because I would not, and, in reality, could not identify those that I thought were my attackers. Finally, he said, "If you think this incident really happened, then we need to get you to the hospital and complete a rape kit."

I was getting pissed off at the idea being presented that the incident didn't really happen. "Well, Captain, the incident really happened three fucking days ago. What the hell good is a rape kit going to do now?"

"You should have reported this when it happened."

"To whom? I had been here less than forty-eight hours when the "welcoming committee" presented themselves. I've heard all of the stories. My goal is to survive this ordeal, get out, and move on."

"Well, we're going to take you to the hospital, and then to the county jail, where you will remain in solitary confinement for your own protection."

"Fine. You do whatever you think is necessary."

I was transported, under guard, to the hospital in handcuffs. I was placed in a room with a guard inside the door, and began a process that was only slightly less humiliating than the incident itself. I now know why women don't report rapes, and I certainly have a tremendous more amount of respect for those that do.

A doctor and nurse came into the room and began collecting "evidence." I was instructed to disrobe, and my clothes were collected on a plastic sheet and put into a bag. Any shred of dignity I still had was about to fly out the window. I was told to bend over the exam table, naked. The door was open, the guard was standing at the door watching, the nurse was watching, and my bare ass was facing the door. A complete rectal exam was performed. A comb that reminded me of one we had used to comb the kid's hair for lice was ran through the hair on my head, chest, and pubic area. Hair samples from each area were cut and plucked so that the roots were intact for testing.

Ever plucked a pubic hair? Damn that hurts. Fingernail and toenail scrapings were taken; swabs from my mouth and every other orifice were taken and cataloged. The doctor wrote down observations and notes throughout the process, although nothing was ever shared with me by either the hospital or the prison. The only comments made by the doctor were that he doubted anything could be obtained almost four days after the incident.

Mild rectal bleeding continued, and after my release from prison, I was diagnosed with an anal fissure---a small tear in the lining of the anal canal. While about 90 percent of these tears heal on their own, occasionally, surgery is required to repair the tear, one of the causes from anal sex. To this day, any mild constipation will cause bleeding.

I was given another orange jump suit, and transported to the county jail. There, following pretty much the same formalities as the prison---paperwork and a strip search---I was placed in confinement. Solitary confinement consisted of an approximate 6' by 6' cell, a bunk on one side, a toilet on the other, and a camera mounted on the wall to watch every movement, including going to the bathroom. There was absolutely no privacy, although I was isolated and alone. I was allowed one hour of exercise per day, which consisted of walking around the cell block. I was allowed to shower, and was actually treated with more respect and less contempt by the County guards than the Federal guards. I could sleep whenever I wanted and was given a book to read. I have to admit, this was the first time I could say that I actually slept since arriving in Yankton, South Dakota.

Several of the prison counselors, the chaplain, and the prison psychiatrist visited during the first two days. It didn't take long to realize that we were playing a game. If I were to say the incident never happened, I could be returned to the Federal prison. If I didn't, there was no telling how long I might be in solitary confinement, or possibly even transferred to another prison facility, all for my own protection of course. The only person that never questioned my accountings of the event was the prison psychiatrist, who merely stated that he would try to help me through all of the issues, and would be more than willing to provide counseling on a regular basis.

I don't remember how long I had been at the county facility when I was instructed that I had a phone call waiting. I was ushered to a room where a county deputy sat across a desk and listened to my phone call. It was my brother, Dave. Since he was an attorney, he said he was representing me and telephone conversations with legal representatives must be put through. Dave said he had been trying to get a hold of me for a couple of days. I tried to explain what had happened, but was overcome with emotion, and I began crying so hard that I found myself unable to talk. Dave spoke encouragingly, and, once again, reinforced God's love for me but that I had to seek God to find it. I assured him that I was certainly going to give it a shot because at this point in my life I had nothing else to lose. I could tell he was upset with all that had transpired, both for me and the fact that he was helpless in doing anything about it. He promised to write and keep in touch.

Finally, following visits with the prison psychiatrist, and two of the inmate counselors, telling them I wanted to return to the general prison population, the recommendation that I be returned to the Federal prison came under one condition: I had to call Joyce, tell her the incident never happened, that I had lied. I agreed to this so that I could move forward and move on. After nine days at the county jail in solitary confinement, I was allowed to return to the Federal prison. In just nine short days, I quickly learned that prison was still very much a closed world, and while within the past two decades TV cameras have occasionally been able to show a very limited view of life behind bars, they have rarely captured anything more than that which the authorities allowed them to see. I thought I could pick up where I left off, but that would not be that case.

I had to start all over, going through the incoming paperwork, strip searches, clothing issue, and bunk assignment. An opening within the education department still existed, so I was able to return to that job assignment. The incident that transpired had certainly been a learning experience. From that point forward, I would have to think through the consequences of even the simplest of daily activities.

Chapter 29

Eventually, I settled into a routine. Although I never got used to the early morning body counts, I used this as an opportunity to read and study the Bible. My eyes were opened to what "life" was really all about. I made a list of goals, beliefs, and values I wanted to work toward, not only during the remainder of my incarceration, but the remainder of my life:

...To understand the mystery of God;

...To know God and know the will of God;

...To know myself and know others;

...To give more than I take;

...To contribute to the well-being and spirit of others;

...To take every chance to help others while on my   earthly journey;

...To seek peace and learn to forgive;

...To be honorable, responsible, and emotionally sincere;

...To truly love those who mean the most and believe that every life I touch will touch me back;

...To have fun, enjoy life, be compassionate, and seek pleasure;

...To face my fears and accept the life lessons of the past;

...To seek wisdom and knowledge, as to avoid suffering caused by my own ignorance;

...To dream again and become the person I've always wanted to be;

...To matter, to count, to stand for something, to
have   made some difference;
…To survive and to live as long as possible.

For the first time in a very long time, I felt that my self-esteem was
gradually increasing, and I began to feel as though I was on the road toward being worthy of love and acceptance again. The prison did have
multiple religious services for every denomination. I attended the
Protestant services, joined the church choir, and attended a Bible study
brought into the prison by one of the local churches. I gave control of my
life over to God; obviously my way didn't work. I had lost everything a
man could lose; only God could restore me to the man He wanted me to
be.

In an attempt to reach my physical improvement goals, I began skip-
ping the evening meal and going to the gym. I started walking on the
treadmill, at first accomplishing only fifteen minutes, but during the next
nine months I worked my way up to running three miles, three times a
week. Additionally, I began playing racquetball and softball. Evenings,
when I didn't go to the gym, I would walk along a circular track that was
interspersed with workout stations for pull-ups, push-ups, sit-ups, etc.
Sunday and Wednesday evenings were spent at the church.

Visitation was allowed on Saturdays and Sundays, and was the one time
each week where we could almost be human again. Within the Federal
prison system, visitors had a lengthy set of "do's and don'ts" to follow.
Not doing so would result in a suspension of visitation privileges, something no one wanted to lose. Based on the first letter of your last name,
family, relatives, or friends could visit on assigned weekend days and holi-
days. Each person visiting must undergo a background check, and be giv-
en approval by the Bureau of Prisons.

Joyce always tried to drive up to Yankton from Sioux City to see me
each weekend. With each visit our relationship changed, for the better.
The lack of physical contact, other than a brief kiss or hug, meant that our
intimacy had to come through our spiritual and emotional growth. Our
feelings for one another became unconditional; we developed this dynam-
ic and powerful energy that we "just knew" would lift us through the
most difficult times, including the baggage of our past lives.

Additionally, I felt that it was going to be extremely important that
Joyce and I share and grow together spiritually. I'm not talking about just

putting on the façade of going to church, praying, and being a Christian on Sundays and Christmas. I was ready for a significant commitment and to put my life into God's hands, but I didn't know if Joyce was ready to do the same. .

I remember, during one of her first visits, I began by reading a Bible verse and asking her thoughts on how it applied to our relationship. I was surprised when she looked at me and said, "We have both been through a lot of trials and tribulations, but my heart is telling me that if our relationship is going to succeed, then we need to experience God together and share what we have learned." From that moment on, my heart and soul opened like a floodgate and we began to share on a new higher level than ever before, bringing both of us out of our comfort zones.

Our emotional intimacy allowed the trust and communication levels between us to reach new highs, and allowed us to broach subjects and cross bridges never before addressed in our relationship. It was unbridled mutual self-disclosure. This was extremely important to both of us, because sadly, it hadn't existed in either of our previous relationships, and ultimately we both paid a very heavy price in having failed relationships. For us, our intimate relationship was to feel wholly accepted, respected, worthy, and even admired in the eyes of one another. We worked to make our relationship a comfortable place for us when we were weary, a place we could find compassion and support.

What Joyce and I discovered during my nine months of incarceration was that emotional intimacy would be the glue that held our union together. We found it was extremely difficult to practice openness and allow one another to be vulnerable to each other. While I know this was a challenge for Joyce, I felt that putting aside my male ego and pride made this a more trying process for me. However, we both struggled immensely with divulging how we really thought and felt, for fear of the ultimate rejection, the rejection of our true selves. It seemed that we were especially afraid of exposing our real selves to someone whose opinion really mattered. I wasn't sure how I would react if I were criticized, laughed at, or seen as undesirable for any reason, due to the baggage of my past.

Together, we came up with a mental list of rules that we agreed to live by so that we could avoid compromising our relationship:

* Spend time alone together each day. Take a minimum of one half-hour each day; it's O.K. to be in each other's company in complete silence.

* Any relationship issues get dealt with when they arise.
* Try to be a person of honesty, character, and integrity in daily life.
* Express your appreciation for your partner with simple, kind gestures.
* Happiness in our relationship and within ourselves is a moment-by-moment choice we continually make. We can control the choices we make.

Chapter 30

Eventually, I was moved to the third floor, in an upper bunk, with a group of men I learned to respect, and they in turn accepted me for who I was. The inmate in the bunk below me, Devin Carr or "D," was, without a doubt, one of the strongest men I had ever seen. He was truly a gentle giant, but had a weight lifting/fitness routine that would put many a pro football player to shame. As an accepted member of this room of inmates, I eventually came to appreciate the loyalty to each other demanded by peer pressure. On more than one occasion, the fact that "D" was my bunkmate and with his prison reputation, I was able to avoid physical confrontation over some other inmate's wants and desires.

The best analogy to describe the day-to-day prison routine would be a comparison to the life of Bill Murray in the 1993 comedy *Groundhog Day*. I found that the daily routine seemed to repeat itself over, and over, and over again. Like Bill Murray's life, prison life forced an ongoing look at the reflection of my own life as seen by others. I was forced to analyze the issues that had resulted in my incarceration, and true to the movie's theme, I was forced to look inside myself and realize that the only satisfaction in life comes from turning outward and concerning oneself with others, rather than concentrating solely on one's own wants and desires. Day-to-day prison life is an unpleasant situation that continually repeats, or seems to, until an individual "gets it right," or at least begins a journey down the right pathway. As a convicted felon in prison, we are exiled from normal life, so we can discover that, in reality, we are exiled from ourselves. Although the movie has a happy ending, only a small percentage of convicts can say the same. Sixty-seven percent of former inmates released from prison will be charged with at least one new serious crime within three years.

It was extremely difficult not to fall into the trap of becoming self-centered. A significant number of inmates always seemed to try and be demanding, controlling, and demonstrate power over family and loved ones. A majority of inmates, especially those that had served a significant amount of time, had all seemed to develop antisocial orientations. They saw crime as the right thing to do, and people were basically objects to be manipulated for their own purposes. Authority figures, in particular, were sources of problems for some of the inmates. While many appeared to establish good relationships with other inmates, they tended to be hostile toward all authority. Thwarting the rules was prevalent, simply to impress a buddy or establish a reputation for toughness. Being exposed to huge amounts of this type of attitude sometimes resulted in my actions and conversations with family not being as pleasant as it should have been.

I remember demanding from Joyce and my kids that they write me at least once or twice a week. After all, it took only about ten minutes to write a letter and there were 1,440 minutes in a day and 10,080 minutes in a week. Wasn't I worth ten minutes of their time? It was flawed thinking; because life in prison was a world within itself, it was easy to forget that life on the outside continued, as did daily work and family demands. Both Joyce and my kids were very good at not letting me sit on my own self-pity pot very long. I remember a couple of telephone conversations that didn't go quite as I had planned.

"Joyce, you don't understand," I bellowed.

"Understand what? That I am supposed to drop everything else that goes on in my life and dedicate every minute to you? Dan, the world doesn't stop while you're in prison."

"All I'm asking is that you write a letter a couple of times per week. Is that too much to ask for?" citing the ten-minute rule stated previously.

"Fine."

Much to my chagrin I received back-to-back letters from Joyce the same day. I anxiously opened the first letter ready to read whatever Joyce had written. Typical of all mail received, the letter had been previously opened, then stapled shut with one staple in the middle of the envelope. I tore open the envelope, pulled out the piece of paper, and opened it with excitement. On the piece of paper one huge letter was written---"A." Confused, I opened the second letter with the same anticipation and excitement, and once again on the piece of paper one huge letter---"S." I returned to my bunk a little perplexed, confused, and admittedly a little angry. As I lay on my bunk pondering what the two letters meant, the light FINALLY went on and I began to laugh until I had tears coming from my eyes.

Later that evening, I called Joyce. "Honey, I got your letters today," with no emotion in my voice; nothing but silence on the other end of the phone. I think Joyce thought I was going to explode.

"If you have five more letters ready to mail, you can forget it. I got the point," laughing uncontrollably.

I heard a sigh of relief on the other end of the phone, and then finally, "You told me I had to write two letters a week, so I sent the first two letters with more to follow if need be," she chuckled.

"Now, that's all right. You write whenever you have time, O.K.?"

"You know I try. Can I come up and see you this weekend?"

"Honey, that would mean the world to me."

Despite the lesson learned it was difficult. I found myself keeping score, the number of letters I wrote versus the number I received from my family and friends. I was afraid that I was "out of sight, out of mind."

The second phone call, within thirty days of my incarceration, with Alisha also grabbed my attention in a manner that hurt, but quickly established the truth about being in prison. I remember talking with Sara about how Alisha was not minding her and acting out. I told her to put Alisha on the phone.

"Alisha, what the hell do you think you're doing? You don't talk to your mom that way."

"Dad, listen to me for a minute and hear my side of the story."

"No, you listen to me! I don't ever want to hear about you talking back to your mom like this again, you got it?"

"Why, what are you gonna do about it from where you're at?" and the phone line went dead; she had hung up. I walked away from the phones with a true feeling of helplessness, knowing that she was right. Just what could I do about it from where I was, and whose fault was it I was here? While both conversations stung, I quickly tried to temper my demands and self-centeredness.

Mom and dad, my brothers, Joyce, and my kids continued to show their support and compassion, despite my stubbornness and determination to make it Dan versus the world. The letters and visitations allowed me to reconnect with life, that for just a few hours would offset the mindless, mundane routine of prison life. It gave me the opportunity to think about life outside the prison walls, to realize that the world does go on, and that I am NOT the center of the universe with my hurts and pains.

Admittedly, my nine months in prison was nothing compared to many of the inmates. Several of the inmates were looking at seven to ten years or longer; still others might not ever leave, or leave in a manner that would truly set them free. It was sad, and yet a majority of those incarcerated accepted their fate and only focused on the mistakes made and what would change the next time. I never have been able to understand those that have been in prison multiple times. I believe it becomes a life style of very little accountability, with a good bed, plenty of food, and guaranteed clothing. For others, I think it allows them to be someone; they have a seniority within the prison walls that doesn't exist for them on the outside.

I truly trusted very few people with whom I was incarcerated. Owen Taylor was another of the few "white-collar" criminals at Yankton Federal prison. He stood probably 6'2" in his socks and reminded me of a college professor. His brown hair was kept in a military style and he wore silver-rimmed glasses that accented the gray hair at the temples. Owen was of stocky build not overweight, but neither was he at his ideal weight. He had a fair complexion, and easily burned in the summer months, which resulted in a reddened face almost as if he was continually flushed with embarrassment.

Owen didn't come across as my idea of the typical banker. He was guilty of allegedly changing banking paperwork to benefit loan applicants. In an effort to help his clients, Owen painted a brighter picture than what may have existed in order to financially qualify for a loan. Despite his efforts to truly help others, Owen's world came crashing down when one of his clients defaulted on a loan that he had assisted them in getting. An audit of the financial dealings with Owen's name on them revealed other questionable banking practices according to the government. Owen had already served a considerable amount of time and had been sentenced to three to five years. He too was assisting in the education department of the prison. We discovered we had a lot in common, both good and bad when it came to why we were at Yankton.

Had we become friends? Yes, of that, I am certain. While most other inmates wanted to talk about themselves and their past, Owen, was willing to take the time and effort to listen and be respectful of what was said. He would make himself available on short notice to listen to any problem, and I worked hard at doing the same for him. I felt that I could tell Owen anything in confidence, and that he was trustworthy. While the relationship developed with a majority of the other inmates was one of just going with the flow, Owen was not afraid of honesty, nor saying what he really thought, even if it meant we agreed to disagree, which occasionally occurred.

Like most inmates, Owen was struggling with his personal and family life. He had already punished himself more that any justice system could invoke. I think it's because of his acceptance of his own bad judgment and poor decision-making, his willingness to accept responsibility and accountability, and his struggles being so similar to mine, we developed a friendship. I hoped the friendship would last beyond Yankton Federal prison, but just as in life, there are no written guarantees.

In early November 2004, I had written and submitted an application for early release to a halfway house based on an Iowa district court decision that would allow it, if good reasoning existed for the early release. Just before Thanksgiving, I was notified that my application had been accepted and I would be released to the halfway house in Council Bluffs, Iowa on December 27. While I was sad that I was going to be in Yankton for Christmas, I was being released to the halfway house a full thirty days prior to my scheduled release date.

Christmas at Yankton Federal prison must have been another page in God's book for the life of Dan Grauer. I truly can't remember a Christmas where I felt so close to God, and so in touch with serving others. The realization that so many other men had spent many, many Christmas Days away from family and friends, that many of the men would live out their lives behind prison walls, and that many of the men truly had no one to share their lives with put into perspective what Christmas was really all about.

On Sunday, December 18, I stood before the church congregation of approximately sixty men, and gave testimony of my mistakes, transgressions, and sins. I talked about the impact it had on my parents, my family, my marriage, and my health. I spoke at length about my prayers being answered when God allowed Joyce Treadway into my life. I related how through Joyce, God gave me a second opportunity to live the life He wanted for all of us. The emotions and feelings throughout my testimony were genuine, and immensely intense. Three times I found myself bawling like a child, and being held and comforted by men whose crimes were deemed abhorrent by society. A full hour later, with God providing the script, I finished with a prayer for each and every man in the prison chapel. As I looked into the faces of the men, you could have heard a pin drop as I believed God had allowed them to truly feel His strength and peace. It was at this very moment, I began to thank God for all I had been through, and for using me as a tool to, hopefully, help others. For the first time in a very long, long time I realized that, despite my misgivings, my mistakes, and my ignorance, God still loved me, and that unlike human love, His is truly unconditional, and that His grace is still available to those that have walked down the wrong path, but found their way home again.

The nine remaining days prior to my departure from Yankton, South Dakota were filled with an unexplainable sense of calm and peace. I had a renewed confidence that life was worth looking forward to and that I had a role in the play of life. I might not like the circumstances, and I might continue to fight the demons of the past, but if I was willing to listen and trust in God, I would be O.K.

Joyce, Tiffany, and Alisha picked me up on December 27 to take me to Council Bluffs. I was instructed to report to the Community Corrections Center, 1228 South Main Street, Council Bluffs, Iowa, no later than 3:00 p.m., or face attempted escape charges. It was made very clear that at 3:01 p.m., unless I had a good reason that didn't even include dying, a warrant would be issued for my arrest if I wasn't standing in front of my assigned counselor.

Simply to be in the car, leaving Yankton, South Dakota, with Joyce driving and my daughters in the back seat, brought forth tears of happiness. For the first time in many years, I felt as though I had a future to look forward to, and I was being accepted for who I truly was.

On the way home, Joyce presented me with yet another surprise. An opening with the State of Iowa Department of Human Services in Pottawattamie County had come vacant doing exactly what she had been doing in Sioux City, and Joyce had transferred to Council Bluffs. I was overwhelmed and honored that she considered me worthy of such a move. She had moved into the Pine Ridge Apartments at 32 Dillman Drive in Council Bluffs. This was a move that placed Joyce a long way outside her comfort zone, and yet she laid her concerns at the feet of God and was content that this was the right decision. I was extremely proud of her. As for me, I prayed that having been stripped of a majority of freedoms that people take for granted, as well as my dignity while literally being forced to fight for the essentials of life, was a chapter now in the past.

Chapter 31

My delusions or naivety of increased freedoms and a new beginning were quickly squashed upon my arrival at the Community Corrections Center. It was not unlike prison itself and I quickly discovered that in many ways, it was worse. The staff at the corrections center did their job according to regulations and standards set by the Bureau of Prisons, but to me, they were glorified babysitters, paid to watch over me like an over-protective mother.

Some of the freedoms behind prison walls were no longer available at the corrections center. For example, in prison, inmates could have over-the-counter medicines and nonnarcotic medications in their lockers. At the corrections center, a Tylenol needed to be requested and documented formally. In prison, going to church or the gym in prison meant signing out on a clipboard; at the corrections center it meant making a request in writing, a week in advance to the director, and hope that it was approved. I have to admit that a vast majority of my requests to workout at the YMCA and go to church with Joyce were granted.

However, I thought that when I left prison I could regain some honor and sense of character, but the mandatory classes beating me down and informing me of how much of a lowlife I was for having caused so much pain and anguish to my family and victims continued. Random drug tests were routine. Locker, bed, and personal effects searches were regular as well. The rooms were almost identical, with as many as eight to ten men per room, with steel-framed, bunk beds, an overly worn mattress or piece of foam, and a locker/basket system for storage of clothing and personal effects.

It only took a few days to understand the reasoning behind the endless rules. The corrections center was coed; women lived on one side of the building separated by the lunch room/visiting room, bathrooms, and staff offices, while the men lived on the other side. The inmates, both men and women, housed at the facility came from all types of Federal prison facilities, from maximum to minimum security. Many of the inmates arrived with horrific attitudes toward authority figures, rule, and life in general. The crimes committed by this population ranged from manslaughter, drug charges, and robbery, to child abuse and pedophilia. Some already knew that this was merely a stepping stone in returning to prison where they felt a sense of belonging, seniority, and not having any accountability or responsibility. Others truly were trying to reform, but had not been provided the tools and coping skills necessary to meet the demands of our society. Many didn't have the education, work ethic, nor skill sets to hold down a job for any length of time, with a majority of the work assignments being menial and simple task oriented.

A good number of the people housed at the corrections center had been "down" for a number of years. The most common rule broken was no fraternization with inmates of the opposite sex. Both the men and women continually abused this privilege, as relationships developed to satisfy the physical needs not met behind prison walls. If caught, this resulted in an immediate return to prison, and many were willing to take that chance. The second most common rule broken was that absolutely no meals from outside the corrections center were to be brought into the facility, supposedly. I witnessed the consumption of more Big Mac's and Whoppers than at anytime during my teenage years. Even I managed to violate this one, sneaking in a full rack of Famous Dave's BBQ ribs to share with those men whose greatest triumph was a hamburger. Getting caught with unauthorized food items usually resulted in hours of additional work tasks, such as scrubbing toilets or showers.

Everyone was required to get a job outside the facility and had jobs assigned within the facility as well. Transportation for filling out job applications, job interviews, and work was limited to walking, bicycling, bus, or being transported by an authorized driver, usually a family member or taxi driver. A time limit was given for completing a job application and, if a person was lucky enough to get a job interview, it was mandatory that you call your assigned counselor during the interview to verify its authenticity. Over time, an inmate could earn driving privileges limited only to work, and the paperwork involved took an enormous amount of time and effort. Proof of ownership, insurance, and a clean driving record was only the beginning in a laundry list of requirements and documentation to obtain this privilege.

Following my acclamation to the routine and my required probationary time at the correction center, I began to seek employment. I knew this was going to be no easy task, and that I would not just pick-up where I "left-off." I had resigned myself to accept whatever employment opportunity presented itself, and make the best of the situation, using it as a stepping stone to a second career. In my mind, I needed to get a job and begin an intense search for a career.

I searched the newspaper ads and employment fliers for anything that would allow me to re-establish some sense of self-worth and self-reliance. I had put together a professional resume to include education, work experience, and business knowledge, but quickly discovered that this was not the pathway to immediate employment. With every application and resume, I was deemed either overqualified for the position for which I was applying, or now having to check "yes" that I was indeed a convicted felon within the last year resulted in immediate disqualification.

Eventually, I read an ad posted by Famous Dave's BBQ Restaurant in the Council Bluffs daily newspaper. They were opening a new store in Council Bluffs and were hiring servers, bartenders, cooks, etc. I had never waited tables in my life, but decided it was something I just knew I could do. Having a base minimum salary plus tips would give me some pocket cash, and if I could establish my business knowledge, I was confident that I could be promoted to assist the franchise in other and more productive ways. I needed to look at each job opportunity as a stepping stone toward a possible career, keeping an open mind with regard to what industry and/or position.

The restaurant itself was located at 50 Arena Way, Council Bluffs, Iowa and was still under construction. A mobile office trailer had been placed just outside the store location and housed the General Manager, Brandon Jones, and several store managers. It was late January 2005, and the wind was vicious and cold. Joyce had, once again, taken some time from her workday to shuttle me from location to location so that I could complete job applications. The task of finding employment was becoming more difficult than either Joyce or I had imagined. I had completed no less than twenty-five job applications throughout the week and was no closer to obtaining employment than the date I arrived at the corrections center.

I walked up the three steel temporary steps, opened the trailer door, quickly stepped inside, and closed the door. Without looking up, a manager named Wayne asked if I was there to fill out a job application. When he did look up, I could see the surprise on his face at my age, but to his credit, he didn't say anything. I was handed an application, and directed to a desk near the far end of the trailer, to a chair just vacated by another hopeful applicant.

It took about ten minutes to complete the application. The process had become second nature, and instead of carrying a resume, I kept a paper with my work history and references for use in filling out the forms. I handed the resume to the General Manager, Brandon Jones. He took a few minutes, looked it over, and then turned in his chair to face me and said, "Dan or Daniel, which do you prefer?"

"Either."

"Dan, just glancing over your application tells me you have way more education and professional background than required for any position we have. What's going on?"

I had made a promise to myself that if asked this question, nothing but the truth would be told, and that's exactly what I did. I did my best to give a truthful, five-minute synopsis of my recent history, my stupidity, and the consequences. I looked Brandon in the eyes the entire time of our conversation. I simply concluded that I had made poor decisions, and suffered the resulting consequences. When I finished, there was a good two minutes of silence before Brandon spoke.

"Well, Dan, I think that each one of us have made mistakes that we aren't proud of. Wayne and Judd, would you agree?"

Both managers shook their heads in agreement.

"I also happen to believe that everyone deserves a second chance to prove themselves. I am going to give you that chance. Consider yourself hired. We are having employee orientation beginning this next Monday across the parking lot at the Country Inn and Suites. I would like you to be there at 8:00 a.m., Monday morning, to begin a two-week training and orientation to Famous Dave's and our expectations."

He stood, shook my hand with a firm, solid grip, and said, "Welcome aboard!"

I was in shock. I stepped out of the trailer and into the cold still in awe. Could this really have been this easy? Or, as I had learned on so many other occasions, was this in God's plan? As I got back into the car, Joyce must have seen the expression on my face and asked, "Well, what happened?"

"I have a job," I whispered.

I looked at her with tears in my eyes and softly repeated, "I have a job." Both Joyce and I were confident that God had once again, through His grace, touched our lives. During this same week, I earned the right to drive a personal vehicle back and forth to work. Slowly, but surely, life was becoming easier and more meaningful once again.

About three months later, Brandon Jones and I had a closed-door conversation, wherein he revealed to me that his father had spent time in prison, and that no one really seemed to give him a second chance. Brandon was adamant that if he could assist someone else by giving them a second chance, he would. His only requirement was that if he chose to give someone a second chance, they had to be willing to change and help themselves as well.

I was determined to give Famous Dave's 110 percent effort, simply because of a general manager and his willingness to give me a second chance without question. Working in customer service proved interesting, and more of a test of my physical endurance than I would have dreamed. It didn't take long to realize that the best opportunity for income was to work during peak times at the restaurant, and in this industry the peak times were the weekends. This meant working as many double shifts as possible, both the day and night shift on Fridays and Saturdays. On many weekends, I came to work on a Friday at 10:00 a.m. and left at 1:00 a.m., only to do it again on Saturday. The upside of these hours was that many nights I walked out of the restaurant not only having earned my wage, but as much as $200 per night in tips. A waiter/waitress willing to work the hours and exceed the customer service expectations of the public could make $28,000 to $30,000 per year.

Brandon Jones continued to provide opportunities and challenges for me as I became more and more familiar with the business objectives, goals, and the restaurant industry. Based on my past, he asked that I put together a training program for the servers that could be utilized at all of the five locations in the Omaha/Council Bluffs area. I was placed on a team that assisted in the opening of new store locations for training and physical set-up, and in October 2005 joined the management-in-training team. Famous Dave's took the training of their managers very seriously, requiring each individual to complete a minimum of six months of training, followed by a mentoring program in one of the assigned facilities.

It was during this time frame I developed the greatest understanding and increased appreciation for the knowledge needed to successfully manage a restaurant franchise. I was required to work in and understand the responsibilities of each and every restaurant position. I spent time cooking, learning how to properly grill the various entrees, and working from recipes to make volumes of coleslaw, soups, desserts, etc. I had to learn the processes for properly smoking the meats, ordering food, the supplies, and financial accountabilities. Famous Dave's expected, and demanded that their managers be proficient from A to Z in their abilities to understand, perform, and manage the processes that had escalated them to one of the most successful BBQ establishments in the United States.

Chapter 32

Having landed a job that required a significant number of hours of work meant that I spent less time at the corrections center, which was O.K. with me. However, it also meant that I provide time slips, accounting for each minute of the day when I was not at the corrections center, and give up sleep to accommodate my assigned job tasks within the facility. I worked hard to stay on the good side of the staff at the corrections center as I had witnessed firsthand the power the staff held in a successful transition back into society.

My relationship with Joyce continued to blossom. We continued going to the YMCA in Council Bluffs two to three nights per week and to church every Sunday. Sharing no more than hug and kiss was sufficient to keep our relationship moving forward, so long as we were right with God, and trusted that our relationship was part of His plan.

Joyce had been attending a Baptist church in South Sioux City and I was a conservative United Methodist. This made for an interesting search to find a church that would accommodate both our spiritual needs and beliefs. Joyce was accustomed to "hellfire and brimstone" preaching, hand waving, and shouting, "Praise God!!" or "AMEN!!" whenever it felt compelling. I, on the other hand, was used to sitting at the pew, singing traditional hymns, and praising God in a more mild, and less energetic manner. We attended several different churches in the Council Bluffs area and found what we deemed a temporary home at Broadway United Methodist Church under the direction of Pastor Brian Landon.

I was scheduled to be released to probation on February 16, 2005 and this presented a huge barrier, in that I had no physical place of residence.

The first requirement of being released from the correction center to a probationary status was proof of an established residence and family support toward continued rehabilitation. The second was established employment and the ability to periodically report to the assigned probation officer for any status changes or updates.

Joyce and I had talked at length and we had both come to the conclusion that I should not move in with her. I think this was something we both desperately wanted and wanted to justify, but could not. Her husband, who was still incarcerated in Texas at the time and not scheduled to be released until 2013, had refused to sign the divorce paperwork presented to him. Consequentially, they were still legally married, and I refused to put Joyce into a position of still being married and living with me. Despite Joyce's acceptance that her marriage had come to an end for numerous valid reasons, Earl refused to recognize the end of their relationship, while continuing to attack her verbally in letters for moving forward with her life. He felt that life could return to what it had been despite his having been convicted on more than one occasion, not accepting responsibility nor accountability for his actions, and having violated Joyce's unconditional trust not once, but twice.

We agreed that when the time was right, and both of us fully believed that God would let us know when the time was indeed right, we would be together. Patience was going to be the ultimate challenge in our relationship during this time. The game plan was for me to at the corrections center until I could afford an apartment, which we estimated would be approximately another sixty days. The downside was that, from my date of scheduled release until I could afford to be on my own, I also would pay rent to the corrections center.

On February 15, 2005, God once again touched our lives with an impact that could only be described as Divine, taking us for a sharp right turn off our perceived straight pathway. The Federal prison in Fort Worth, Texas, notified Earl's brother, who had called Emmylee, Joyce's daughter, on Wednesday morning February 16, that Earl had suffered a massive heart attack and had died on Tuesday. Joyce was in a state of disbelief and denial. She was extremely saddened at how her marriage of over twenty years had ended, and yet, she appeared relieved that Earl could be at peace and no longer struggle with his own inner battles and with his struggles of societal acceptance.

She cried, remembering the good times they had while raising three wonderful children, while allowing Earl's family members to live with them in order to help out, and the good memories of Earl himself and their early marriage days. It was obvious that they had once shared in a caring, loving, and trusting relationship. The best I could do was to offer an emotional shoulder, encourage her to hang on to the happy memories, and assist with any funeral arrangements.

Over the next few days, I encouraged Joyce to spend time with her children, and to take her time in making the funeral and burial arrangements. Unfortunately, Earl's untimely death got caught up in the Bureau of Prisons' bureaucracy. While the Bureau of Prisons agreed to do the embalming and provide the casket, transporting his body to Sioux City, Iowa had become a challenge. Because he had died while in custody, the Bureau of Prisons insisted on doing an autopsy as well. Joyce discovered that a multitude of rules and regulations existed for transporting Earl's body, to include the fact that only certain airports could accept the deceased. The best arrangement she could make was to fly his body into Omaha, Nebraska, and have the funeral home transport his body to the burial location. Ten days later, Earl's body arrived in Omaha and was transported to Sioux City, Iowa. The visitation, funeral, and burial arrangements were made for the evening of February 25 and 26.

I had planned on staying at the corrections center for whatever additional time was necessary; however, on Thursday, February 17, while exercising at the YMCA, Joyce asked me to move into her apartment. I had not broached the subject given the recent series of events in her life; however, we spent the evening discussing the pros and cons of this scenario.

We knew that we were going to marry, but didn't know when. We agreed to keep separate finances until such time it made sense to combine them, but financially, overall, it would be less strain for both of us.

We had hid nothing from our children regarding our relationship and the expectations for our future together. The spiritual, mental, and emotional stability that we afforded each other far outweighed any negative we could think of. In a discussion with our Pastor, he said, "While I can't support living together prior to marriage, Dan, you and Joyce are already married; it's simply a matter of holding the celebration".

We were comfortable with ourselves and we recognized that we each had something important to contribute to our relationship. We loved one another for who we were and not the idealization of one another. We each wanted more than anything to help one another grow in every aspect of life.

While accepting that intimacy, passion, and commitment were essential to our relationship, we were also realistic enough to know we need to continuously work to make it successful. Finally, based on our previous relationships, it was extremely important to both of us that we could NEVER take our relationship for granted.

When it came time for Joyce to drop me off at the corrections center, we had agreed to take another huge step in our relationship. Although I was somewhat uncomfortable with the timing, I was confident that our lives were being blended by a higher power, and for the first time, in a very long while, was able to dream about the future. I only know that when I walked through the door of the corrections center that evening, I felt as though I was walking in the clouds and wore a grin from ear to ear.

Chapter 33

Finally, on February 21, 2005, I left the corrections center for home. It had been a long, long time since I could even reference having a home. During my ten months of incarceration, I had tried to define what a home should be: "home" should be not only the physical place you hang your hat every evening, but also a place where you find shelter, protection, safety, and relief. This should be that special place in your house where you feel most comfortable, like a comfy chair where you can kick your feet up and let all your cares slip away.

I believe a home should also include the person who comforts and supports you most. That person, for me, was God's gift to me: Joyce Treadway. With Joyce, I felt that I could be completely me and that's a part of being home. Home is having that special someone who understands that I would struggle with the dark and light inside me, and never pass judgment when the dark occasionally wins the battle. Hom is sharing my safe place, a place where I can go for complete and utter acceptance, and, at the end of the day, I can rest my head on her shoulder and feel completely at peace. She is my refuge, my home in this earthly world. As I walked down toward Joyce's car, tears streamed down my face; I did indeed have a home once again.

As I walked, a prison memory flashed into my mind. I remembered a particularly difficult time when I was struggling with life behind bars, a man by the name of Buck Alexander, the prison choir director, a convicted felon himself with a down time to date of seventeen plus years, told me, "Let the hurt fade into the dark and let the good times shine through. When you're positive and happy, people respond in a positive happy way, too. Life is always going to hand you lemons in some form or another, so make lemonade. If it's sour, add more sugar, 'cause we all could use a little more sweetness in our lives. And if it still doesn't taste right, toss it...and start anew. Just never give up being YOU, 'cause even when you feel those bumps and bruises, there is someone out there who thinks you are mighty damn fine!" This was one of those pieces of advice that would be easier said than done, but a worthy goal none-the-less.

During the remaining days prior to Earl's funeral, I encouraged Joyce and her kids to spend some time etching and cherishing the memories of Earl into their minds. I encouraged them to look at photographs and to take photographs at the funeral. As a family, they had been separated for so long, the good memories needed to be documented.

While displaying a conditional acceptance of our relationship, Joyce's children were extremely leery about letting me into their lives. For so long, it had been the Treadways versus the world that the concept of dissolving the team was illusive to each of them, including Joyce in many aspects. I had vowed to never let them forget their father, nor would I ever pretend to take his place. I believed it was important for them to create a ceremony that reflected who Earl was and their lives as a family, their shared ideas, beliefs, and feelings.

Joyce was worried about the financial arrangements for Earl's funeral. Earl's brother and Joyce's children couldn't contribute much, and Joyce didn't have enough in her savings or 401(k). As we discussed her fears and concerns, I tried to comfort her with what we had learned during the past ten months: to trust in God, and give it up to Him for handling. I assured Joyce that together we could take care of any financial obligation she felt appropriate in order to provide the needed comfort to her family. Admittedly, I was secretly happy that the need to trust in God and move forward was in someone else's court for a change. I wondered if Joyce could be as good of patient as she was a doctor.

"Dan, I can't let you help pay for my ex-husband's funeral," she said.

"Honey, it's not about money. This is about a significant portion of your past, and the fact that you need to do this for you and your kids. We have opened our arms to one another and established a partnership, that means we are willing to accept all of the baggage that came attached with our pasts."

"Are you sure?"

"Yes, I am. I didn't know Earl. What I do know is that you have treasured, happy memories, of time with him, that he is the father of your kids, and that if I am any kind of Christian at all, I need to do what is right, and this feels right."

The funeral was memorable and they picked out a very nice headstone for Earl's grave. Most of Earl's family was able to attend the funeral, and he was laid to rest beside his mother in a ceremony that was satisfying to both Joyce and the kids.

Chapter 34

From the end of February 2005 through November 2005, life had its ups and downs for both Joyce and I. We quickly discovered that sharing our lives was going to take plenty of work and patience. As partners, our physical, spiritual, and mental relationship was awesome, but the baggage from our scattered pasts continued to haunt us both.

In an attempt to make right our past financial negligence, we uncovered about $11,000 in past debt from Joyce's side, and about $4,000 in past debt from my side, and that didn't even include the $240,000 in restitution I was ordered to pay as a result of my conviction.

Personally, I struggled mentally with the return of my male pride. It was even more complicated because I was not sure who I was within society, or what I wanted out of life. Additionally, it was foreign to me having someone I could weather the storms of life with when things got tough, and I wasn't familiar with being able to forgive, forget, or the resolve to move forward when issues arose. However, Joyce continued to accept me as I was and tried really hard not to change me, allowing me to learn from my own mistakes and grow. We had numerous discussions regarding the fact that only time and God can change someone, if that person is willing and open to change.

As we moved forward trying our best to live the Christian life, we were discovering the blessings and gifts also continued. Monies and refunds from sources we had long forgotten suddenly appeared in the mail, relieving some of the financial burden.

During Memorial Day weekend of 2005, Joyce and I were strolling through Wal-Mart, getting groceries and doing some serious window shopping when I was overcome with an idea or a feeling that I was compelled to act upon. I know that Wal-Mart is not the fancy-schmancy jewelry store that many couples wanting to get married shop at, and Joyce and I were on an extremely tight budget, but my heart unleashed a barrage of emotions that allowed me to send Joyce into an unexpected state of "flabbergast."

To this day I don't know what made me do it, but I walked up to Joyce as she was standing at the jewelry counter gawking at rings, got down on one knee, grabbed her hand, and asked, "Joyce Ida, what seems a long time ago I made a promise to your father. I believe with all my heart the time is here. Will you marry me?"

Of course, Joyce immediately starts crying and says, "Dan, are you sure?"

"I have never been more sure of anything in my entire life. We have gone through so much, both as individuals and as a couple, and I'm sure I have some baggage that may sneak up on us yet, but God brought us together for a reason. I think it's time for us thank him. What do you think?"

"Yes, I would be honored to be your partner."

Out of the corner of my eye, I caught a movement that made me glance from Joyce's eyes to the clerk standing behind the jewelry counter just in time to see her dabbing at her eyes with a Kleenex. I asked the clerk, "What are you crying about? You're going to make a sale of a diamond ring." Everyone in the immediate area began to chuckle.

Joyce and I then proceeded to pick out a very modest, but unique, engagement ring that represented our love for one another. Our bedtime prayer was spent hand in hand simply thanking God for all of the blessings and gifts. We spent the next two hours merely cuddling and talking about our future and our dreams, knowing that we could survive anything that came our way. I don't recall anytime during the past several years where I had been as happy, content, and confident that my life was finally headed in the right direction.

Chapter 35

Despite my advancements through Famous Dave's BBQ, I continued to keep an updated resume and apply for various careers where I could utilize my business management, risk management, and business operations experiences and skills. Joyce and I were on opposite shifts and were becoming a little distraught with her working 8:30 a.m. to 4:30 p.m. and my hours being 4:00 p.m. to midnight, or later. Finding a career was going to be an uphill battle. Many times, I was eliminated for consideration for employment on the cursory review of my application; checking "yes" to have you been convicted of a felony in the last twelve months appeared to be a death sentence. However, having struggled with patience in the past, I was determined to persevere this time.

And as the story says, "lo and behold" despite all that God had done for us, He was there once again. Joyce and I turned to Him for guidance and direction, vowing to live according to His plan. I mean, after all, who would be more qualified to give guidance than one who had already been on the same road and arrived at His destination perfectly?

In late November 2005, I was introduced to Kylie Jordon, founder of Excellence Personnel, and Dusty Fisher, founder of Downtown Staffing. I later discovered these ladies had a mother/daughter relationship. Both ladies immediately presented themselves as devout Christians. While focusing on different clientele, each outwardly demonstrated an entrepreneurial spirit, including attributes such as courage, dignity, wisdom, and strength, with an innate ability to put anyone at ease, promote confidence, and reassurance that a career could be found. Neither woman batted an eye or flinched when I unloaded the story of my past. Instead, they focused on the positive and provided words of encouragement, mixed with the honesty and frankness that it would not be easy.

We massaged and tweaked my resume to place the emphasis on my accomplishments and what strengths we felt that I could bring to any corporation. While a majority of her concentration was on the blue-collar worker, Dusty did an extensive amount of work with people recently released from prison and/or jail, and had contacts with various employers to fill relatively labor intensive jobs. She was quickly establishing herself as a successful entrepreneur in the employment industry.

Throughout numerous discussions, she continued to amaze me with her innovative and trailblazing ideas. Dusty was willing to take a justifiable risk and not necessarily play it safe, and certainly was not close-minded about how to increase her chances of success. She had the ability to take a single idea and focus on it for maximum potential rather than be diluted with hundreds of half-baked ideas. As a business professional, she had experienced a setback or two, but elected to soldier on through it all, pick up the pieces, and start again; to me this took courage and determination. I remember her telling me, "Too many people give up if they make a mistake. Only a few are prepared to learn from them and turn them to their advantage."

Kylie appeared to focus more on white-collar employment and seemed to have openings from accounting/bookkeeping through senior management. She had carved a niche into the employment world that resulted in a service that could ease a pain, fulfill a dream, make life easier, or make life better for both employee and employer. She came across as extremely organized and committed to her business. Kylie would set goals for herself and her clientele, then back it with a burning desire that rubbed off on even the laziest of career seekers. I believe this attribute alone contributed to her success when other employment agencies were struggling; she had the ability to swim upstream. There was a synergy created between Kylie and her clients that seemed to harness the power of diversity, unlock true potential, and empower all of those in need toward meeting a common ground and creating a win-win solution.

Sometime during the week of December 5, Kylie called and asked how much warehouse operations and/or quality experience I had. We discussed how my past in risk management integrated with quality, as both assessed business processes, but from a different angle of the business. We spoke about my operations experience and how I felt my business knowledge and experience could be applied to the operations requirements she had listed. She told me that a corporation by the name of Bluffs Telecommunications was looking to fill two positions, one as a Quality Engineer and one as an Operations Manager. Kylie truly felt that I could be successful at both and asked permission to forward my resume to them. I agreed, but held my breath, thinking that this might be one more time when my hopes were dashed by my past.

Following our phone conversation, I did some Internet research on Bluffs Telecommunications and found they had an impressive track record in the reuse and repair of telecommunications equipment. They had some major clients that held controlling interests in the telecommunications industry as a whole, and they appeared to be on a pathway of expansion. I found out what I could about CEO Hayden Jackson and VP of Operations, Tyler Martins. Tyler Martins was located in the Council Bluffs facility and had been in the business a relatively short time, transitioning when Total Communications became part of Bluffs Telecommunications. He had been in his current position since 2002, overseeing the warehousing, fulfillment, and distribution services.

From reading his biography, Hayden Jackson appeared to be an expert in acquisitions and growth. He had been at Bluffs Telecommunications since early 2000 and, holding true to his expertise, led the transformation of four entrepreneurial entities into one integrated operation.

My research led me to believe that Bluffs Telecommunications was working toward goals of building a great company in the next generation by solidifying the current foundation. In a recent business leadership class, I learned that great companies get the right people on the bus and the wrong people off the bus before they figure out where to drive it; Bluffs Telecommunications was doing this. By researching their leadership teams and their history, it appeared that Bluffs Telecommunications placed greater weight on character than education, skills, or experience when hiring. Any corporation can teach skills, but character, basic intelligence, work ethic, and dedication to fulfilling commitments are values that are ingrained in a person. Their acquisitions appeared rigorous, but not ruthless. I would be honored to work at Bluffs Telecommunications, but vowed not to get my hopes up. The first step was to get an interview, and for this I relied on Kylie.

I don't remember what day in early December Kylie called and informed me that I had an interview. I would have a team interview with

Molly James, Manager of Human Resources, Tyler Martins, VP of Operations, Andrew Thompson, Warehouse Director, and Angela Crane, Executive Assistant to Tyler Martins.

I felt that Tyler Martins would be the key to landing this career, and the more I knew about Tyler the better off I would be. Kylie had told me that Tyler was a former state patrolman, and had taken some classes at Harvard prior to taking over at Bluffs Telecom. Through further research and by making a few phone calls I formed the following opinions:

1. Tyler Martins appeared to have a high need for self-determination.
2. Like most successful executives he had a unique distaste for feeling controlled or manipulated.
3. He was described as having a personal commitment to what he did and had that need to have a "sense of ownership."
4. Tyler Martins was characterized like many of the successful individuals I was honored to work for in that: They believe that they have the motivation and ability to change their world. They see success for themselves and others as largely a function of motivation and ability, not luck, random chance, or external factors.
5. I learned that he would communicate with an overall sense of self-confidence almost to the point of intimidation.
6. Finally, I believed that Tyler Martins was a high achiever and like most people that are, because they have achieved results, they tend to believe that they were instrumental in helping the results get achieved, and this is true more often than not.

One day prior to my interview, I called Kylie to strategize how to handle the more difficult job interview questions I anticipated. I told Kylie that I would not lie to anyone at Bluffs Telecom if asked about my past. She concurred, but stated that an interview was also like talking with the IRS: only answer what is asked of you.

I had come too far not to put this into God's hands. I was just now beginning to recognize that there are times when the struggle is intense. Submitting to God may involve cost or sacrifice, but He'll have something far better for us in the future. I was finally learning that it's always best to yield to God's perfect will for one's life. I was wholeheartedly convinced that if working at Bluffs Telecom was what God wanted me to do, it would turn out to be the very best life for me.

I left Bluffs Telecommunications feeling really good about my first professional interview in a very long time. I felt that I had accomplished all my objectives: I had researched the company, remained confident, focused on my main strengths and skills while selling myself as an asset to Bluffs Telecommunications, had prepared knowledgeable and appropriate questions for the interviewers, and I was relaxed.

At no time during the interview was I asked significant questions about my past. I volunteered that I was terminated from the railroad and ended my response. I expected someone to follow-up with the dreaded why question, for which I was prepared to tell the truth; to my amazement no one brought it up. It was then that I was more confident than ever that God was with me during the interview. I truly felt that I could be a good fit at Bluffs Telecommunications if given the opportunity.

Little did I know just how difficult that would be: I endured five interviews with multiple managers and senior managers. I was tempted to ask about being put on the payroll simply because I had been inside the Bluffs Telecom facility so frequently that I was beginning to know the front office staff by first name. However, on February 17, 2006, I was finally offered the position of Quality Engineer. I agreed to an annual salary and benefits, plus I would be required to attain several Quality certificates, while hitting the ground running and prove myself by utilizing my business, risk management, and operations skill sets to make a positive difference at Bluffs Telecom. Working within the Quality department would allow me to have a direct impact on the company business processes. I was certain that Bluffs Telecom was no different that other companies I had worked for in that every company has some processes; some are clearly defined, others are implicit. Success means to increase productivity and reduce costs while generating the same or better outcomes. I believed that Bluffs Telecom understood the need to continuously improve their business processes, to become more efficient and productive, and to respond to market changes faster while providing better service to customers within the telecommunications industry, and that alone was exciting.

My personal life was looking brighter as well. In April 2006, Joyce and I purchased a house. We both had the desire to create an environment of security and happiness that we could call ours and have a dwelling that truly represented who we had become. We had our first real home together. Joyce and I knew that our union was one of God's making, but we still fought the problem of trust: trusting that God's abundance was meant for us, trusting that we didn't need to do it all alone, and trusting that God would provide.

We did have our share of challenges, trials, and tribulations as we attempted to merge our families. At one point, during the summer of 2006, we had nine people and three dogs living under our roof. It wasn't until we started setting and enforcing some rules and boundaries that our children, (ranging in age from nineteen to twenty-five), started to accept the accountabilities and responsibilities that come with growing up. With some gentle prodding, they found new residences and/or jobs, finally daring to leave the nest. For Joyce's children, the transition to living on their own seemed less dramatic because of what they had endured in their past and because they each had previously lived on their own.

We had wanted to get married in the spring or fall, but when my ex-wife set her wedding date for May 10, I was not about to turn getting married into a competition. Joyce and I agreed that we would wait until the fall and set a date of September 23, 2006. We planned a small wedding, fewer than seventy-five people, to be held on the dock at Boy Scout Island on Lake Manawa. Because it was a second wedding for both of us, we wanted to make it informal and simple. Our goal was simple; we wanted to be able to look back on our wedding day with a sincere fondness, knowing that we were brought together by His magnificent grace and glory. That thought alone instilled a sense of comfort that no matter what we chose to do for a celebration, it would be enjoyable and memorable.

From May 2006 through September 22, 2006, Joyce and I worked hard at living out our pledge to one another, taking all that life had to throw at us and reframing it into something positive. By taking the time to focus and notice what's right, we could watch the world change in front of our very eyes. Learning to be grateful allowed us both to be open to the abundance of joy and happiness that surrounded us when we looked for it. We remembered how happy we were as kids and allowed ourselves the silliness of acting like a kid and playing like a kid on occasion.

Given our pasts, even during the worst of times, we discovered that kindness is contagious, and when we make a commitment to be kind to ourselves and to others, we can experience new heights of joy, happiness, and enthusiasm for our lives. We learned that to be in the moment is to live in the moment. We would try to catch ourselves when thinking ahead

234

or looking ahead to the next event or circumstance in our lives, not appreciating the here and now. I think that when we savor every moment, we are savoring the happiness in our lives.

We learned that there are times when we need the time to unwind, decompress, or, simply put, to just chill. Through our freedom of choice and decision-making, life comes at all of us hard and fast. Time, just like the days on the calendar, keeps going forward at its own natural pace, which is not always the pace we would choose. Fatigue, stress, and exhaustion may begin to settle in on us faster than we may think or notice. An afternoon of cuddling, listening to music, or watching a movie allowed us to recharge and rest.

I had spent the last several years learning that sometimes we have to fake it until we make it. I learned that it's extremely important to be honest, real, and authentic with others, but I also learned that, at times, we just need to put on a happy face and keep moving forward. Finally, because of failed past relationships, I believe we learned that it's important to know when to say when. What gives you joy and happiness the first time may not work the second time. Too much of a good thing may begin not to feel as good if the "thing" becomes more of a routine, or an expectation, or unhealthy. Together, we learned to set healthy and reasonable boundaries for ourselves and we continue to work at trying not to overdo it.

September 23, 2006 didn't give us the exact weather we were looking for. The weather was cloudy and cold with a light mist coming down, but none of that mattered because this was the very beginning of a new chapter in my life and end of another. The inscription on our wedding bands stated it best: By His Grace is how we planned to live our lives. And so, with the two that gave me their unconditional love, loyalty, and believed in me most, we officially came together as one family. K.C., my black lab, led the way as he strolled proudly down the aisle with our wedding rings attached to his collar, occasionally stopping to say "hello" to those he knew, followed by my very own angel, Joyce Ida Treadway. My whole world was changing for the better. I couldn't help but grin from ear to ear as I looked deep into Joyce's eyes, and through the tears sang to her from my heart, "Keeper of the Stars," by Tracy Byrd:

It was no accident me finding you
Someone had a hand in it

Long before we ever knew
Now I just can't believe you're in my life
Heavens smilin' down on me
As I look at you tonight

I tip my hat to the keeper of the stars
He sure knew what he was doin'
When he joined these two hearts
I hold everything
When I hold you in my arms
I've got all I'll ever need
Thanks to the keeper of the stars

Soft moonlight on your face, oh how you shine
It takes my breath away
Just to look into your eyes
I know I don't deserve an "angel" like you
There really are no words
To show my gratitude

So I tip my hat to the keeper of the stars
He sure knew what he was doin'
When he joined these two hearts
I hold everything
When I hold you in my arms
I've got all I'll ever need
Thanks to the keeper of the stars

It was no accident me finding you
Someone had a hand in it
Long before we ever knew

Acknowledgments

I would like to acknowledge those people who have provided ongoing support and strength throughout this entire ordeal, and without whom my earthly existence would have ended long ago:

Mom and Dad

My brothers (Dave, Doug, and Dennis)

My children (Ryan, Tiffany, and Alisha)

Joyce Grauer (my current wife and partner in Christ)

But most of all:

"Thank you, God, for your patience, wisdom, gentleness, and forgiveness in allowing me to get through this most humbling experience, and to come closer to you! Amen."

About the Author

Dan Grauer, Sr. Quality Engineer at a major telecommunications corporation went to prison for the poor decision-making from his past. He has presented keynote speeches, workshops, and seminars to high schools, colleges, church organizations, and community organizations regarding "white-collar" crime and money addiction. Dan's goal is to keep others from making similar poor life choices.

Dan lives in Council Bluffs, Iowa with his wife and two dogs. He is very active in his church and hopes to enter the ministry full-time at some point in the future. This is his first novel.

36922914R00136

Made in the USA
San Bernardino, CA
06 August 2016